Richard Rowe

Passages from the Diary of an early Methodist

Richard Rowe

Passages from the Diary of an early Methodist

ISBN/EAN: 9783337163341

Printed in Europe, USA, Canada, Australia, Japan

Cover: Foto ©ninafisch / pixelio.de

More available books at **www.hansebooks.com**

PASSAGES FROM

THE DIARY OF AN EARLY METHODIST

By the late RICHARD ROWE

WITH A PREFACE BY

THOMAS PERCIVAL BUNTING

STRAHAN AND COMPANY LIMITED
34, PATERNOSTER ROW, LONDON

Second Edition.

PREFACE.

IT is little more than two months since the lamented author of the following pages ended his comparatively short career of modest and meritorious labour. His name never became famous; he was wont to conceal it when he addressed the public. But he occupied no mean rank among that useful and influential body of writers, who, of late years, have availed themselves of the facilities afforded by various serial publications, and have thus done much to sustain, enliven, and purify the literature of the age. The story of his chequered life, and of its pathetic close is admirably told in the "Day of Rest," for February, 1880.

That story explains the secret of his success as an author. Whether Art seek to realize the ideal, or to idealize the real, the power and habit of minute and accurate observation supply the main element of success. Truth—truth only—or the very likeness of it, touches the instincts and the sympathies of men. No fancy, however glowing, no power of picturesque detail, can permanently affect us by an impossibility. A child is ever asking, "Is it true?" And the mature man is best satisfied when he says within himself,—"This may have been, perhaps has been, perhaps *is* true somewhere?"

This faculty of careful observation was possessed in no ordinary measure by Richard Rowe.

In the present "Diary" he had to make himself full master of the past of a sect whose history, until very recently, has commanded little general attention. Contemporaries of its earliest adherents knew, and cared to know, as little about them as we do of the thoughts and habits of modern Jews. In the present case the knowledge was very easy of acquirement. The writer was the son of a "Methodist Preacher," of the average type, and of an epoch extending during some portion of the half century which immediately succeeded John Wesley's death. No great leader of men ever left a deeper impress on his followers, and if Rowe's father never saw Wesley, he must have held large converse with those who lovingly remembered, and were accustomed to relate, "the traditions of the elders." In the days, also, of which I am now speaking, converts, new and old, were put upon reading, and they read with avidity, "The Journals" and "The Minutes," with their quaint but solemn record of departed worthies, and lively biographies, as natural as they were gracious, and, above all, the "Old Magazines"—those same "Old Mad Methodist Magazines," as Charlotte Brontë called them—the confessed inspirers of her genius, and the sources of intelligence to thousands of readers throughout the world. Thoughtful men studied them, and clowns and dullards were kindled by them into a reverent sympathy with former times. It is plain that Richard Rowe had industriously mined among books like these. The itinerant life of his father, too, must have brought him within ready reach of very various details of the information he wanted. Notwithstanding the common and conscious brotherhood of all the members of the sect, there was a wide difference between the London merchant or the Manchester manufacturer, and the fisherman of Cornwall or the pitman of Newcastle.

We find no distinct picture in the "Diary" of the earlier "Methodist Preacher," properly so called. Poor Pidgeon made a disastrous failure in his attempt to join that rank, and remained distinctively a layman. But of this latter class he is a perfect sample. There were—I may safely say there are—men who exactly answer to the description. If there be a difference, it arises from the fact that the original wears an air of sadness and anxiety which only persecution and care can stamp on any visage. These were and are those who, under the power of one great impulse, never knew or know any other which it does not modify, control, and sanctify; men with more or less of earthly culture—sometimes with the highest; but all with intensified affections upward and around; heedfully treading the "narrow" way, and, not so commonly as may be supposed, with any narrowness of aim or spirit. Indeed, who so broad and catholic?

Think of the grand old Methodist driven from house and home by one of such a clergy as Macaulay describes,—a brutal and irreligious hireling, heading mobs, or sneakingly countenancing them; hunting his victim into poverty and shame, and sometimes to a violent death. And if he survive, where do the two next meet? Not where justice sits, but beneath the shadow of the well-accustomed parish church, where one of them, at least, joins, heart and soul, in confession of his sin, and in prayers for his "enemies, persecutors, and slanderers," and then hears "meekly" a furious declamation against all he knows in his deepest consciousness to be good and true. Puritans and Quakers in their turn had suffered, though not so much; but suffering had driven them into quite another course. Truly these "trees of the Lord were full of sap."

On the other hand, who that knows Methodism, past or present, fails to recognize the typical Saunders? Very desirous—using the Methodist vernacular—"to flee from the wrath to come," as being, even to a worldly mind, an issue much to be deprecated; yet, in the very same spirit, a devout worshipper of Mammon; provoked to transitory "love" and occasional "good works" by ceaseless counsels from the brethren, and the steady influence of a good wife; never daring to renounce his connection even with the sect everywhere spoken against; but inconstant, shabby, mean, and grasping.

There are two respects in which, as it seems to me, these pages cast a stronger light upon the earliest Methodism than has been shed by any—of course excepting the two Wesleys, in their respective published "Journals"—who have hitherto contributed to its history. Pidgeon, though with much more precision and fulness of language, writes very much in the general style of the Nonconformist of a century before his time. There is the truth of art in this conception. Not so much, perhaps, in the larger centres of population, as in the smaller towns, and in obscure corners of the land, the Puritan movement had hardly languished out before the new revival, adding fresh fuel to the expiring embers, lit up a lively flame ; and, in some respects, the nursling of Puritanism came to be the nurse and mother of modern Nonconformity. The young, strong Methodism, in countless instances, where Puritanism had not abjured its ancient faiths, rushed to the help of the decaying churches, supplied them and their off-shoots with vigorous pastors and agents; and laid the foundations of their present numerical and religious greatness. Dr. Halley, in his noble History of Lancashire Nonconformity, has copiously illustrated this interesting subject. Isaac Watts knew little what he was about when he expostulated with Doddridge, because the latter evinced so much sympathy with Wesley and his work, and even hinted that he was in danger of losing the funds which sustained the Academy at Northampton.

And, again, this book brings to the light another fact which has almost gone out of mind. I refer to the imputations so commonly cast upon Wesley and his first adherents of disloyalty to the House of Hanover. No wonder the common people were willing enough to credit these absurd scandals. And, to be fair, even thoughtful men may be forgiven, if they suspected the new movement of political associations and aims. The father of the Wesleys had been nourished in Dissent; had, at a time when the prospects of the Georgian dynasty were still obscure, become a somewhat conspicuous Conformist; and had wavered between Jacobitism and the Low Churchmanship of the time, with a vacillation which nothing but his poverty can excuse. Now sprang up the sons; Samuel, the eldest, a pronounced politician, with the highest ecclesiastical opinions; and two others, John and Charles, prodigies of zeal, shaking the kingdom with views so old as to have been forgotten and so to appear as new; and proposing to set up an organisation within the very bosom of the Church, such as had never hitherto been thought of. There was a haze hanging about the whole matter which only time could dissipate.

The writer's sketches of Wesley himself are exceedingly life-like, with the one exception that none but Wesley could command the terse vigour of his epistolary style. That he should have been grieved at Mr. Pidgeon's failures during his short itinerancy, and at his ultimate abandonment of it, was natural enough. The more sagacious a man has found out himself to be, the more he is mortified when some clear demonstration of unwisdom stares him in the face. For the rest, Wesley stands out in his native dignity, sweetness, and strength; an erring man, indeed, but of heroic purpose, commanding will, exquisite charm of manners and demeanour, boundless resource, and, above all, resolute fidelity to his extraordinary vocation. It is doubtful whether his biography will ever be fitly written. Any grateful adherent of his system may, most probably, be fettered by either the partiality, or the dread of it, which have characterised former attempts. Would that Robert Southey, when he essayed the task, and with so much success, had been of the number of Wesley's elect disciples!

The "Diarist" deals largely and characteristically with the supernatural and the spiritual. Otherwise he had been no true Methodist of his time. Methodism was nothing if it was not intensely spiritual; and the otherwise supernatural shaped its form and life. Perhaps it was that they who had so suddenly and overpoweringly been brought under the sway of the unaccustomed and unseen contracted a somewhat morbid appetite for the marvellous. Perhaps there *were* marvels obvious to inquiring eyes, but to none other. It may be that the strong light confused the sight, and transformed the object on which it shone. At all events, this age must not laugh at them—this gaping, gasping, and wondergreedy age! A few years' residence in some foreign Roman Catholic village ensures, pretty certainly, a sight of the Blessed Virgin, and probably a cure for the quinsey. Ghosts are to be seen and heard, nearer at hand. And, as to the sacred mysteries of the inner life, —the mysteries that concern our relations to God and with Him—amiable and, in some sense, honest Deists have their "experiences" too, and fancy they have found their way into His favouring presence without the mediation of His atoning Son, and the help of His revealing Spirit.

I have not commended this book to the reader. Let it commend itself. One of its highest merits is its suggestiveness. But, when its beautiful pages shall have been exhausted, let me recommend the various other publications of Richard Rowe. They are true to nature and to life, picturesque in grouping and detail, and often specially pathetic. Charles Dickens never wrote a finer passage than the description of "Old Tim," in " Dr. Pertwee's Patients."

T. PERCIVAL BUNTING.

CHISLEHURST, *February*, 1880.

I.

1744—Jan. 26.

THE New Year hath begun in a new way with me. Hitherto it hath been my pleasure to think, as each came round, that I was increasing in wisdom and in favour with God and man. I was happy in my wife and children, and in good repute among my neighbours. No man, methought, could lay aught to my charge. My school hath steadily increased in numbers ever since I first settled here, and this I looked upon as a sign that my labours were approved in Heaven. I paid my way, like an honest man, out of the fruits of my own toil. I led a spotless life, and strove hard to teach my children, my scholars, and my servants to lead the same. Never did I say, because never did I think, "What lack I yet?" With my lips I called myself in church a miserable sinner, but 'twas a mere fashion of words. My heart asked for no mercy, because it felt no need of any. Rather I gave thanks that I was not as other men, extortioners, unjust, adulterers. And now all is changed. Yesterday, John Britton, the exciseman, persuaded me to walk with him to Bath to hear Mr. John Wesley preach. It was not that I had great curiosity to hear him, or respect for his person. I had looked upon him as a turbulent tinker among parsons, going about the country making a disturbance, because he had not gifts and patience to render him respected in a settled cure of souls. It had been whispered to me likewise that he was in foreign pay, a Jesuit in disguise; that in all England, yea, Scotland and Ireland, King George had no worse enemy than he. I had taxed Britton, inasmuch as he took the king's pay, with double disloyalty in following such a man; and I fear I had taken unseemly delight in noting how little effect the faith of which poor John prates hath had upon his behaviour. It was to triumph over John by holding up to scorn the very words of his teacher, so that he might have no excuse in lack of memory, that I went with him to Bath.

Mr. Wesley took for his text the General Epistle of James, second chapter, latter part of fourteenth verse, "Can faith save him?" Sure, thought I, if he had searched the Bible through, he could scarce have found a text worse fitted for his purpose. Doth not the Apostle say before, "What doth it profit, my brethren, though a man say he hath faith, and have not works?"

And after, "Faith, if it hath not works, is dead, being alone."

But, to my wonder, Mr. Wesley waxed warm on behalf of works, and it was odd to see John Britton's astonished face. But my turn soon came. Mr. Wesley next made light of works alone, and was, moreover, so severe in his judgment of what might entitle works to be called good, that, at the last, it seemed to me that I had neither faith nor works to save me. He spoke much, too, of a holiness without which, as a wedding garment, no one should see God, but of which I knew nothing; so that the pains of hell gat hold upon me. And there were many moved. A gentlewoman, who had come dressed for the Rooms in her fine hat and feather, trembled so that I could see the seat shake, and sobbed aloud. As we walked home by the flooded river it minded me of the swelling flood of which Dr. Watts sings, with no sweet fields beyond for me. Nor yet can I read my title clear. My mind is strangely disturbed; I can but strive to enter in at the strait gate, with no assurance that I shall ever see the other side. Yet, Lord, I do believe; help Thou my unbelief.

Feb. 1.—Thanks be unto God, which giveth us the victory through our Lord Jesus Christ. This morning, after I had wrestled with Him in prayer for three hours, He spake peace to my soul. It had been borne in upon me that if I did not hear the pardoning voice before the clock struck seven, I should be lost to all eternity; and when the clock on the stairs began to warn, and I was still unsaved, the hair of my flesh stood up. But before the church clock had finished striking, I could claim Jesus as my Saviour. O day ever to be remembered!

Wed. 8.—My light still shineth clear, and the cup of my joy would run over, could I but bring those of my own household to fall with me before the Mercy Seat. But the veil is not yet lifted from their hearts. When I speak, they wonder, as though I told them idle tales. The sure Rock of my salvation to them is but a sick man's dream. They hold me in too much reverence to treat me as Christian was treated by his friends, but 'tis plain that they look upon me as one half distraught. When at prayers this morning, finding the printed words too strait to utter the fulness of my heart, I burst forth in thanksgiving of my own, it cut me to the quick to see the look which my wife cast upon me. Oh, could she taste the joys I know! Oh, could they all! Could all mankind!

Thurs. 23.—Having made bold to write to Mr. John Wesley, to tell him of the great things which the Lord hath done for my soul, and at the same time of my exceeding sorrow on account of those near and dear unto me according to the ties of the flesh, I have received from him a letter (of which the following is a copy) writ, it would seem, in London, but despatched from Uxbridge :—

"DEAR BROTHER,—I rejoice with them that do rejoice, and weep with them that weep. Cast all your care upon God, for He careth for you. Truly these are days in which we ought to humble ourselves under His mighty hand. Hourly we expect to hear that the French have landed. It is for our exceeding wickedness that we are thus threatened, but, peradventure, God may yet be prevailed upon to turn away His wrath from us as He did from Nineveh. In this Nineveh, in which there are thousands who will not discern between the right hand and the left in the way of well-doing, and who follow their lusts more brutishly than their cattle, we have held a day of solemn fasting and prayer, and to make it such a fast as the Lord would choose, our people have dealt bread to the hungry and covered the naked. In this time of searching of hearts I have good hope of the speedy deliverance of your kindred. Let your light so shine that they may glorify your Father which is in heaven. He is able to save to the uttermost. May ye soon comfort one another with these words.—J. W."

II.

Fri. Feb. 24..

AM now openly called Methodist, because I have not shrunk from assembling with the one or two who meet together in the name of Jesus, and find Him in their midst. We have not yet suffered persecution, but I know not what may come, more especially if our numbers increase. And sure 'tis my duty to strive to bring others to the knowledge of the truth, which hath proved so blessed to myself. The Rector hath spoken to me. "Why canst not be content, Pidgeon," said his Reverence, "to go on teaching thy school steadily as thou hast always taught it heretofore? Read thy prayers, and welcome, an' thou wilt, but I will have no praying without book, and preaching of strange doctrines to the boys. Sure my sermons are good enough for thee. Come to church when other decent folk come, and don't bother thy head about being righteous overmuch. See

what comes of it. The exciseman hath been drunker than ever, ever since he took to saving his soul. He'll lose his place. I'd not forbid a man to get merry over his ale—thou'dst be all the better for it, Pidgeon—so long as he could carry it, but Britton is past bearing. Then this getting up in the dark, and meeting together after dark—what is it for, Pidgeon? A few Squires hereabouts may have thy wishes, but mark me, they'll not back thee if it comes to trouble. I'm a King George's man, and won't help a traitor. The scholars I got thee, I can take away—mark that!" And away he went, walking ankle over in the mud, and cracking his whip, as his manner is when he is angry.

'Tis true what he saith about the boys. I may say without boasting that my school is better taught than any other in these parts; but they who sent me their sons on the strength of Dr. Green's good word, if he took it from me, would not stop to think of that. After he had gone my wife burst into tears, and said, "Mr. Pidgeon, sure, you will not take the bread out of our mouths for a mere crazy whim. You are no rebel at heart, I know full well. If you do not care for me, think of your children, Nathaniel." It is Sarah's talk of this kind that makes my burden doubly hard to bear. Oh, could we see eye to eye! But the treasures for which, methinks, however hard might be the trial, I could now sacrifice anything, are spiritually discerned. As for this idle talk about Mr. John Wesley being in the pay of the Pretender, if they who spread abroad the rumours would but hear him, they would learn that 'tis other kingdoms than that of this world he careth for, that the warfare he hath enlisted in is not between King George and King James, but our Lord Jesus Christ and the devil.

Sat. 25.—Mr. Knowles, the steward, who hath been into Staffordshire on his master's business, rode up and had a talk with me after morning school.

"What's this I hear, Pidgeon?" he said. "*You* turned Methodee—that's a Vrenchman and a Papist! D'ye want to kiss the Pope's great toe, and eat vrogz and wear wooden zhoes? D—— me, but I thought thou'dst more o' the zperrit of a free-born Englishman. We wunt have no brass warming-pans here, I can tell ee—bundle ye all into the horse-pond, if ye don't mend your ways—zarve ye as the volk I come from zarve ye."

And then, with many oaths and much boasting, he told me that the Staffordshire gentry (believing that idle tale about the Pretender!) had sworn that the Methodists should no longer be suffered to insult the Church of England and plot against the king, and had mustered an army of men by the castle at Darlaston, who vowed they would drown every Methodist in Trent. 'Twas strange to hear Mr. Knowles brag of the abominable way in which the mob abused poor women.

All the Monday night they were mustering, and drinking themselves madder even than blind rage had made them (for what knew they of the doctrines of those they went about to kill, yea, had bound themselves by oath so to do?), and on Shrove Tuesday they marched in on Wednesbury. Giving their bulls and cocks a little rest, they came to bait and shy at the Methodists. All their goods the mob spoiled, out of wanton malice destroying what they could not or would not take away. Not a window pane was left in a Methodist's house; the very frames were torn out. Food was thrown into the street, and trodden into mire, good bread and beef and cheese. Furniture was broken up, and piled for fires; of clothing they carried off what pleased them, men in their drunkenness putting on women's attire. Beds were dragged from under women big with child, and when they had been ripped up, the feathers scattered to the wind. Men had to flee for their lives, and women in fear of worse than death. Lord, what is man that thou regardest him? The little children were left to shift for themselves, like young birds flung from a harried nest. I marvelled to hear Mr. Knowles, whom I had looked upon as a man of a kind heart, rejoicing over these things, and threatening us with the like. So hath the evil one blinded his eyes!

And then, forsooth, the gentry who had set the mob on, sent word to the fugitives that they might have back what was left of their goods, if they would promise neither to hear nor house the Methodist preachers more.

Meanwhile the mob went round about the country wrecking; not always, from what Mr. Knowles unwittingly let drop, harming Methodists only, but taking all quiet folk who could not help themselves for such. Some of these, it seems, at a place called Aldridge, they ducked in a big pool, who fled into Walsall, and gave the alarm. And so when the mob came to Walsall, the gentry there, of a different kidney from them of Wednesbury, set upon the ruffians with a chosen band, and took from them their fresh plunder, which afterwards was restored to such owners of it as could be found. Mr. Knowles vaunts that the Methodists were for the most part too terrified to claim the remnant of their goods. How long shall sinners thus furiously rage? O Lord, give me strength both to do and to bear Thy will.

Thurs. March 1.—Passing the Brass Knocker, Mr. Knowles threw up the window, and called me in. I had no wish to enter, judging from the redness of his face and thickness of his voice that he had already drunk too much, though I had but just dismissed my school. Here, alas, 'twould clear no man from the charge of drunkenness to point out that it was but the third hour of the day; and by the sixth many are stupid or raging. Nevertheless, being determined, so long as I could do so with a good conscience, to abstain from giving offence to Mr. Knowles, since his word is all-powerful with my Lord, I went in. I found the Steward sitting in the Sun, with the landlord and the curate of ——. All three had been drinking hard, and two of them were very noisy, but for Sam Noakes, save at last to make him drowsy when 'tis time to shut up, his ale hath no power over him. They had been discussing affairs of State, and passing a tankard towards me, bade me with many oaths drink the health of King George, and d—— to the Pretender. Now though the calling of toasts hath always seemed to me a foolish custom, invented to give men excuse for tippling, I thought I might without offence wet my lips with the ale, and wish long life to my Sovereign, but the other part of the toast, as being unchristian and profane, I would not drink. Thereupon they all set on me, declaring me a rebel.

"Rare news hath come from London," cried the Steward. "King George hath bundled out all the Papishes, with thy Jack Wesley at their head, and we'll not stand a scum of fellows that turns the stomach of the Londoners. John Britton will never gauge another barrel, let me tell thee, and if thou'lt not leave thy Methodee ways, out ye all go, and thou'lt not find another roof in this parish, nay, nor four parishes round, to cover 'ee, I can tell thee."

It is very true what he says, and I can but pray that he may have spoken in jest, for if I lose my house, and cannot get another near, I shall lose my scholars also. And how am I suddenly to find a new livelihood? Our little savings would soon be spent, and then we must live upon our furniture, and what should we do when that was gone? O Lord, direct my steps. Strengthen my heart, that I prove not false to the faith through fear of man.

Fri. 2.—I have appealed from Philip drunk to Philip sober, but 'twas of no avail. Mr. Knowles tells me plainly that I must take my choice, give up my house, or else give up the Methodists. On my return, I met John Britton starting for Bristol. It is true that he hath been discharged, and he tells us that the Steward is resolved to drive out all our little band by Lady Day. "I'll harry their nests," he boasts. 'Tis not law, but if we appealed to my Lord, he would stand by his unjust steward; and what can humble folk such as we are do against a great man like my Lord? Poor John would fain have had me tarry to drink a pint of ale with him, but of that, alas! he had already had 'enough. 'Tis strange he hath sacrificed his living for his faith, and yet will not sacrifice to it his lust, thus bringing reproach upon the people of the Lord, and Him who hath called us.

Sun. 4.—The Rector took for his text 1 Peter ii. 17— " Fear God. Honour the king," and preached as though the Methodists did neither. He was determined, he said, to do his best to root out from his parish sneaking rebellion and popery in disguise. 'Twould have been well if he had had a word to say on the first part of the verse, " Honour all men." This open denunciation of us hath soon told on the baser sort in the village. With the Rector and the Steward both against us, they know that they are not likely to be called to account for their behaviour towards us. Mud was thrown at the windows during our evening meeting : and when we came out we were hustled by a mob. This is, indeed, but light affliction compared with the persecutions which some are called to endure, and yet 'tis hard to be made little of by the lowest, where aforetime I have been looked upon with respect by all. Some, too, who would not join with the rabble, looked on as if they thought we were served right, and none interfered on our behalf. Perchance,'tis not wonderful, after what the Rector had said of us, though I make bold to answer that we are as true

Englishmen as they that are set against us, and stauncher churchmen than the bulk of them. How often do they go to the church they express their readiness to die for? We must expect things harder than mud soon to be thrown against our windows, and ourselves likewise. It grieves me that through me my family should be exposed to outrage, and yet, should it come upon us, 'twould be easier to bear if they could rejoice therein. "Blessed are ye when men shall revile you, and persecute you, and shall say all manner of evil against you falsely for my sake." Lord, open Thou their eyes, and let us be one fold under one shepherd.

Tues. 6.—I have had another visit from the Rector, and he, like the Steward, saith I must take my choice. If I will not give up the Methodists, he will take away my boys. He hath already another schoolmaster in his eye, ready to step into my shoes. The Doctor had been talking to my wife before I went in, and she joined her entreaties and reproaches to his stern rebukes to prevail upon me to forsake my purpose. Following their mother, the children, too, looked coldly upon me. It is hard for flesh to bear. "Thy wife hath twenty times thy wit, Pidgeon," said the Rector, as he took his leave. "I am sorry, for her sake and the children's. But I can't part man and wife. Whom God hath joined let no man put asunder. As you sow, you will reap. The fathers have

AN EARLY METHODIST.

eaten sour grapes, and the children's teeth are set on edge. You must support your family as best you can. I shall bid the parents of the boys to send them to the new schoolmaster. The sooner you're gone the better. Anyhow, Knowles tells me he means to turn thee out at the quarter. And mark me, Pidgeon, if I hear of any tampering with the boys whilst thou still teachest the school, I'll commit thee to County Gaol as sure as I'm a Justice."

Sat. 17.—I have been glad of the half-holiday after a week's work, but now it but brings to my mind how soon my work here will be done. A good half of my scholars have already left me. Their parents have sent in word that they can trust their sons no longer with me, and of these most have sent but a part of the money for the quarter's schooling, while some, taking advantage of the Rector's displeasure against me, have sent none. And the lads who still come are strangely altered in their behaviour. They know how I am spoken of, and some of the bigger openly deride me. The little lads, moreover, to whom I have been as a father, mock me behind my back. They point the finger of scorn at me, and call me Methodist. My little Jack must needs dare Joe Collins, though much bigger than he, to fight him for so doing. I rebuked the boy, but could not find it in my heart to chastise him. I trust that the pleasure I took in finding one of my own flesh still true to me was not sinful. The others, with their mother, look upon me as their undoer. It is idle to hope that I can tarry longer here. Mr. Knowles told me yesterday that, whether I chose to continue Methodist or not, I must, for my obstinacy, turn out on the Monday after next, inasmuch as he hath let the house over my head to the Rector's new schoolmaster. He hath no right; nevertheless he spake as if he did me favour in suffering me to remain until the Monday, because Lady-day falls this year on a Sunday. Next week I must seek some lodging for my family.

Thurs. 22.—My school is broken up. A few of the lads seemed to take it to heart when they bade me farewell. Their parents have been more just in their payments than were those of the lads who first left. A few said that, if they durst, they would gladly still send me their sons. But, indeed, where should I receive them, unless I kept school, as I have heard they do in Ireland, under a hedge? and then, doubtless, if it were anywhere on my Lord's estate, Mr. Knowles would send the constable to disperse us. Squire Wilton sent for me and offered me a cottage rent free on his estate, but when I found that 'twas from his attachment to the exiled Family, and because he thought I was likewise disaffected to his Majesty, I thanked him and said, Nay; affirming that no men were more steadily attached than Methodists to his Majesty's royal person and illustrious house. "Ay, but which Majesty?" quoth he, wondering. "King George," said I. Whereat he cursed me for a fool, and himself for another, and bade me go about my business. However, I have hired a lodging to which we depart on Monday. As yet I have heard of nothing for our maintenance, but I will trust to the Lord to provide. Who am I that I should murmur? "Foxes have holes, and the birds of the air have nests, but the Son of Man had not where to lay His head."

Good Friday.—This morning at church, in the reading of the Psalms, it seemed as if these words were made for me: "But I am a worm, and no man; a reproach of men, and despised of the people. All they that see me laugh me to scorn: they shoot out the lip, they shake the head, saying, He trusted on the Lord that he would deliver him, seeing he delighted in him. But be not thou far from me, O Lord: O my strength, haste thee to help me."

Easter Sunday.—Alas, this hath been a day of drunkenness and riot! Thus do men praise our God for His goodness in raising our Lord from the grave for their redemption. In coming from church in the morning we were insulted, and should have been evil entreated, had not Sam Shaw, the blacksmith, not so drunken as the rest, abashed the mob. "Nay," quoth he, "let the poor women and children be. 'Tis no fault of theirs." So the rabble contented themselves with hooting us to our home, and vowing vengeance on me, whom they called the sneaking Popish spy, when I had not my wife's petticoat to hide behind. "What hath he to do in our church," they cried, "but to spy how he may best bring in the Pope and the Pretender?" And not one of these Church of England men, I will be bound to say, had been inside the church that morning, and many of them not for many a day. "For all thy wife and brats," they shouted, as they departed, "we'll drag thee through the horsepond, Pidgeon, if we catch thee here another Sunday." All this was hard for flesh to bear, especially for my poor wife, who hath taken great pride in the good name which she and all belonging to her have hitherto borne in the parish. We sat at home all the afternoon, not daring again to go to church. 'Twas grievous to see my own flesh and blood all glooming at me, all save little Jack. "Father," quoth he, doubling his little fist, "I would have fought for thee."

It seemed as if all love for me had died out of my wife's stony face, but when I was starting for our evening meeting, she threw her arms around me and wept, beseeching me not to go forth. It was the first time she had kissed me for many days, and to please her I would fain have tarried at home, had I not called to mind Daniel kneeling in his chamber with windows open three times a day towards Jerusalem, although threatened with the den of lions. "Whosoever, therefore, shall be ashamed of me and of my words in this adulterous and sinful generation, of him also shall the Son of Man be ashamed, when he cometh in the glory of his Father with the holy angels." Those solemn words came likewise to my mind, and, taking up my cross, I went out. There were very few at our place of meeting, most of our little band, terrified by the threats of the Steward, having looked back after putting their hands to the plough. And not for long were we allowed to enjoy the comfort of Christian fellowship. The windows were broken, and we were forced to flee for our lives. The place is quiet now, and all my people are abed. This is the last night that I shall sleep in this house, to which I came full of hope, and in which, till of late, have lived in good repute; to which I brought my poor wife, in which all my dear children have been born. No more shall I delve in my garden, wherein the buds and flowers are opening. O Lord, increase my faith.

III.

Sat. Mar. 31.

WE have been now nigh upon a week in our new home, though verily it doth not yet seem such. The chambers are small and strange, and as I know not how soon we may have to leave, 'tis but as though, after long tarrying in a familiar haven, we had cast anchor for a single night upon a troublous voyage. I had not believed Mr. Knowles to have been so hard of heart. Sure, he might have been content with unlawfully turning my poor children out of their home like young birds from their nest, but, peradventure, 'twas because his conscience pricked him that he raged the more furiously. Howbeit, he brought and set the mob upon us when we left on Monday. These pious keepers of Easter, having filled themselves with strong drink (many of them, 'twas plain, had not been abed all night, and could scarce keep their legs), came with their fiddles, their whistles, their bells, pans, cleavers, and confused tumult of voices, and flung addled, stinking eggs, mire, and dung at us as we rode forth upon the waggon, the steward egging them on, cracking his whip, and bidding us with many oaths begone, as if we had not as much right as he upon the king's highway. "Raging waves of the sea, foaming out their own shame. Like the troubled sea when it cannot rest, whose waters cast up mire and dirt." And not content with this, they flung stones. We were wounded in person, our goods and apparel were much damaged, and my face burned like a hot coal at the beastly talk the ruffians did not scruple to utter in the hearing of my wife and children. I know not how far the devil might have driven them, had not the Lord sent the Rector to deliver us out of their hands. Just then one of the crowd had snatched from my little Susan her bird, which she had brought away in its wicker cage, and wrung its neck, swearing in his drunken folly that it should sing no Methodee hymns. At the sight of his sister's tears my little Jack, clenching his fists, would have leaped from the cart upon the fellow, had I not restrained him. The Rector likewise had seen it all, and coming up bade the crowd begone for cowards, and rebuked Mr. Knowles for the countenance he gave them in molesting women and children. And when, encouraged by his saucy answer, the mob still lingered, the doctor laid on lustily with his whip, and sent them scampering. Then having spoken a word of comfort to my poor wife, and patted Jack upon the head, he bade me a gruff good-morrow, and saith to the waggoner, " Drive on ;" riding at a little distance behind us, until we were safe out of his parish.

I fear I have moved here to but little purpose. The parson tells me that if I attempt to open school in his parish, he will summon me to appear before the Spiritual Court for teaching without licence. It was graciously given unto me in that hour what to say, and boldness to utter it.

"Sir," I answered, "we must all appear before the Judge who sitteth upon the great white throne, and, when the earth and the heaven have fled away, and the dead, small and great, stand before God, and the books are opened and the dead are judged out of those things written in the books, what will He say unto them who would fain have starved their fellow-men for no other crime than wishing to spread abroad His most holy name? 'Inasmuch as ye have done it unto one of the least of these my brethren, ye have done it unto me.'" For awhile the young man was abashed, but he soon gave me "Saucy fellow" again, and, when I would have reasoned with him, broke into open rage. "Had I my way," quoth he, "I would make short work with your Methodists—bundle them aboard a man-of-war, make soldiers of them, make slaves of them, make mincemeat of them. Not one of them should be out of gaol, waiting his turn of the gallows. What business have such canting, scheming rascals to live? I'd as lief knock a Methodist on the head as I would a rat; the pestilential vermin!"

It was strange to see this young gentleman, who hath been bred at the University, and taken upon himself the ministry of the Prince of Peace, foaming at the mouth like a mad dog, as he uttered this wild gibberish, almost choking in his rage. 'Tis well he is not in the Commission of the Peace! What judgments might we expect from a justice who scrupleth not to say that he would willingly commit murder! Fortunately, the people of the village are a quiet folk, who set small store by their firebrand parson. But, alas, they are utterly dead to spiritual things—no ditchwater more stagnant—they care for none of them. It is borne in upon me that my soul will not be free from blood-guiltiness if I shrink from speaking a word to them in public of Him who hath done such great things for my soul, and is able and willing to save to the uttermost all who come unto Him in faith. Praise to His name, in this my time of temporal darkness, my soul is filled with His light. The love of God is shed abroad in my heart by the Holy Ghost given unto me, and perfect love hath cast out fear. No more spirit of bondage, but the Spirit of adoption. The Spirit beareth witness with my spirit that I am a child of God. Oh, that my dear wife and children were but sharers in the same blessed salvation! I hate sin with a perfect hatred, and have completely conquered it.

Sun. April 1.—" Let him that thinketh he standeth take heed lest he fall." For the saving of my soul I have been most mercifully brought to shame. After writing in my diary last night, I spent, according to custom, some time in private meditation, then read God's Holy Word, and offered prayer and praise to Him upon my knees, my soul still unclouded; and in that happy frame of mind I fell asleep. 'Twas strange, then, it might seem to some,—but, indeed, I recognise in the vision the good hand of God,—that I should have had a frightful dream. Methought that I came up with Christian and Hopeful as they talked with Ignorance, and joined with them in rebuking his folly and presumption. Nevertheless, he would not answer me roundly as he answered them, and when they went upon their way would fain have had me tarry to be his companion. Indignantly I answered Nay, and pressed on to the abundant delights of the country of Beulah. As I sat there in an orchard, listening to the voice of the turtle, suddenly, as is the manner of dreams, the sun for a moment was darkened, and I beheld Ignorance being hurried through the air overhead by two who were not Shining Ones, but angels of the devil. Following on foot to see what should become of him, I saw the door in the side of the hill, which in the Pilgrim's Progress is called the by-way to hell; and when it was opened, I heard the roaring of the fire and the cries of the tormented. Into this gulf the dark ones threw Ignorance, and afterwards seized me to cast me in likewise, but with a cry of terror I awoke. My hair was wet with the sweat of my fright, which ran down my face and neck in big drops as cold as though I had plunged my head into a pond. When I had told my wife the reason of my outcry, " Nay, Nathaniel," she saith, " 'tis plain the dream is sent to tell thee that thy present ways are wrong. Thou hadst quiet sleep while thou wert content to be an honest man, before thou hadst grown so righteous overmuch that thou must set thyself up above thy betters, and bring thy family to beggary. What is to become of us, I know not. Thou wilt get no scholars, and thou seekest for no other work, as if an idle life pleased thee. Though who would hire a headstrong man like thee, that has given up a comfortable home for his whimsies? I would fain work for my poor children—though sure 'tis the husband's part to keep his own flesh and blood—but thou heardest what the rector said, Nathaniel. None would give me work neither, because thou'rt tied on to us like a stone.

Don't tell me that's religion. I like religion that can pay its way, and keep a roof over them that belong to it, instead of being content to see 'em starve, so long as you can shut yourself up quiet, and fancy fiddlesticks. 'Tis not behaviour worthy of the name of a man, Nathaniel, and so I tell thee plainly. I'm not to be made to hold my tongue, if my poor children are to be left to starve. What doth the Bible say? I know so much of it, thank God—'If any provide not for his own house, he is worse than an infidel.'" These bitter words were exceeding hard to bear. I had not misdoubted it during our courtship; but since we became one flesh, I have found that my dear wife hath a sharp tongue. During the time of our temporal well-being she curbed it, and ever treated me in public with respect. But now at times she raileth at me openly before the children, as though I were a drunkard, or an idle fellow that wilfully neglected her and them. 'Twould be cruel should she turn away from me their love. I fear not as yet for my little Susan and my little Jack. Yet even they regard me otherwise than they did, as one who hath done some wrong, they know not what, which they will nevertheless forgive, out of their love for me, and because of the anger towards me of others. And this is not the way in which a mother should bring her children to look upon their father. What with her words and my dream, I was much discomposed until I had called to mind my blessed experience of the night before, and felt that my trust still stood firm in the Lord. As for the dream, though bad dreams will long hang about one like a bad odour or a bad taste in the mouth, I had pretty nigh worked it off for the present by the time I went to morning service. I have made up my mind not to forsake my parish church, whoever may minister therein; but by regular attendance thereat, to put to shame them that falsely accuse us of being traitors to our church and king. But it was a trial of patience to have to listen to the Vicar. Verily I pitied his poor people as he emptied before them his boyish jumble of dry scraps, like stale crusts from a beggar's wallet. But it seemed to matter little to them what 'twas they heard, if not too long. Verily my heart burned within me to rouse them to a sense of their state as sinners, and of the free salvation awaiting them. Therefore, when I saw them coming out of their cottages after dinner, altho' the wind blew keen, and hail had rattled against the church windows in the morning, I went out, my family much wondering what I was about, and invited them to assemble under the gable of our little house that I might speak a word in season unto them. Many came; and though snow had begun to fall ('tis strangely cold for this season of the year), joined with me in the singing of a psalm, but when I had given out my text,

"Jesus Christ the same yesterday, and to-day, and for ever" (Heb. xiii. 8), my eyes chanced to fall on the Vicar's face quietly watching us. I verily believe that the devil had entered into him, for the fashion of his countenance was altered. His face no longer wore its wonted foolish aspect as of an overgrown lad, but a malignant sneer as of a fiend.

Instantly my dream returned to me, and it was borne in upon me that Ignorance had good right to claim me for companion, and that the devil, knowing this, had come to mock me for my presumption in thrusting myself forward as a teacher. The words I would have uttered froze upon my lips, and, seeing this, the devil, by the mouth of the Vicar, shouted, "Dumb dog, April fool, pelt him home, boys." Covered with shame, I fled, indeed, like a hunted cur, to the scorn of my wife, and confusion of my children. Having gained my chamber, I fell upon my knees, and poured out my heart before God, praying Him to strengthen and enlighten me. Here I have ever since remained. My wife hath retired to rest · with her elder daughters. Of all my family Susan and Jack only came to the door to bid me good night. It pricked me to the heart that little Susan shrank from me when I kissed her, as if half in fear.

Mon. 2.—O Lord, lift Thou up again the light of Thy countenance upon me. My soul is passing through deep waters. Oh, suffer Thou not me to sink therein, as one who hath no hope. I fain would be Thy true disciple, did I but know the way. Oh, let me feel again, to the salvation of my soul, and the comfort of my heart, that Thou art the Way, the Truth, the Life. How long, O Lord, how long wilt Thou be angry against my prayer? Thou feedest me with bread of tears, and givest me tears to drink in great measure. My enemies laugh among themselves. Turn me again, O God of hosts, and cause Thy face to shine, and I shall be saved. O Lord, fulfil Thy promise. My sins are as scarlet. Make them white as the snow that now lieth round me on the hills."

IV.

Wed. April 11.

AFTER a dreary time of doubt and waiting I can again rejoice in the Lord. The winter is past, the clouds have lifted, and I again behold the clear shining of the Sun of Righteousness. The time of the singing of birds is come. And on this balmy evening, after long cold rain, 'twould seem as if the material world had made itself a mirror for my soul. The grass and the young leaves are all aglow. The cuckoo is crying in the wood. The pear tree is coming out in the garden. This day I brought my little ones home a nosegay of wild flowers. They seem to have sprung suddenly out of the ground; and had there before been flowers to gather, I had not had until to-day the heart to gather them. For days I had been miserable as the man with an unclean spirit in the country of the Gadarenes, who had his dwelling among the tombs. Always, night and day, my soul had been in the mountains and in the tombs, crying and cutting herself with stones. The devil stood ever at my elbow, walked with me step by step, mouthing at me, and saying, "Since thou knowest one of thy blessed experiences hath proved naught, a burst soap bubble, why may not all that thou hast had, all that thou, perchance, mayst have in future, be as fond? What is thy religion but thy mood? When thou thinkest thyself ripe for heaven, mayst thou not be rotten for thy fall into the jaws of hell?" And when I strove to pray, he told me it was waste of breath. "As thou must come to me at last," he whispered, "eat, drink, and be merry, or else leap at once and be damned. Sure hell cannot be worse than thy present wretchedness." 'Twas on Hampton Cliffs I plainly heard him say, "Cast thyself down, and see who's right. Pray while thou fallest, an thou wilt, for God to deliver thee." And with a mocking laugh which rang in my ears, although the hill gave back no echo, he urged me to the brink, and had I not suddenly sprung back two yards and more, I should most certainly have dashed myself to the bottom. Since yesterday se'nnight, rising early and returning late, hiding myself from my own flesh and hanging my head like a bulrush, I had gone forth and wandered round about upon the hills, finding all both within and without dark and cold. But this morning when I went out before sunrise, the air felt milder, and as the sun came up, I had for the first time for many days, a passing gleam of hope. Clouds continued to float across the sky during the forenoon, but the air waxed warmer and warmer, and by one the sun had chased away the clouds. As I stood on Landsdown, a voice said to me, "Cross the valley, and when thou seest cause for prayer, pray, and if thy prayer be answered, thy faith will return, and thy heart shall be once more like that of a little child." So I went down into the city, and toiled up the hills on the other side until I came to the quarries at Coombe Down. As I looked down into them, lo, a horse drawing an unloaded truck ran away, and in its path a little child was lying. I could give no help, save to fall on my knees with a cry of, "O God, save it!" And it was saved. The horse sprang over it, and the truck striking against a big block of stone, bounded over it likewise, coming down within an inch of its little outstretched hand. At the sight of this miraculous interposition of Providence, my faith in the efficacy of prayer immediately returned. The eyes and the lips of my blind, dumb soul were opened by the same Ephphatha, and when the mother had picked up her infant, I retired into a cranny of the rocks, and poured out my heart before God, who graciously again spake peace to my soul. Everlasting glory to Thy name, O

Lord! On my road homeward, glad of heart, I gathered for my little ones their nosegay, and when they saw my altered countenance, they ran out to meet me as of old. My wife likewise noticed the change and smiled, thinking that I had heard of employment. Poor woman, 'twas sad to note the cloud that came over her face when she found her disappointment. The peace which I have regained and treasure as a pearl of great price, to her is but as the Pilgrims' truth to the people of Vanity Fair. Lord, open Thou her eyes. Nevertheless, our present mode of life must be a cross unto her. I will bestir myself.

Thurs. 12.—The Vicar called to ask why I was not at church yesterday, and took upon himself to say that my absenting myself on the occasion of a Public Fast was manifest proof of the disloyalty of my principles in matters both of Church and State. 'Tis unfortunate, but he would but have mocked, had I explained how this came about.

Fri. 13.—I have received great comfort from communion with the brethren in Bath. Brother Saunders, who hath the big shop in Southgate Street, hath, moreover, promised me employment as accountant. I am very thankful, and would judge no man harshly. Nevertheless, I cannot but think that I should have received a larger wage had I less freely opened my circumstances. Mr. Saunders is in pressing need of a good accountant, and, without vanity, I may reckon myself such. 'Tis not, therefore, a deed of charity he does, although he would so have it. But why should I behold the mote in my brother's eye? I render hearty thanks unto the Lord for this merciful opening of His Providence. In course of time I may obtain more lucrative employment, and, meanwhile, my wage will support my family with care and economy, and in prudent management my dear wife was never lacking; which is strange, inasmuch as her father was a curate, and after having suffered much want in her home, she was suddenly exposed to the temptation of waste when she became maid in a great man's house. My little ones must go to the dame's school, and the elder ones, still learning, prepare their tasks for me to hear on my return to my home.

Mem.—To hear little Sukey and Jack read likewise, and to see that they are not suffered to fall back in their cyphering. This house being cheap and near the city, I shall (D.V.) remain here. The walk out and in will be of service to my health, and give me opportunity for meditation. My wife is glad, but would have been better pleased had not my employer been a Methodist. She says that he hath not promised me enough to recompense me fairly for my toil; and this, indeed, is true; and that I shall be made the more obstinate in my ways of thinking through my service in his house. 'Tis these opportunities of Christian fellowship which have contented me with the poor pay. Although not of a liberal spirit, brother Saunders hath a great gift in prayer.

Sun. 15.—'Tis strange the change one week can bring about. This day se'nnight I was prisoner to Giant Despair, and now my cup runneth over. To-morrow I go to my new employment. I have had a most peaceful day. There hath been more concord and kindliness among us than there hath been since the day when the Lord opened my eyes. O God, let not this be a snare unto me. Bring my beloved ones to a knowledge of the truth, that we may, indeed, enjoy fellowship, the communion of saints. In his sermon this morning, the Vicar could not let poor Mr. John Wesley alone. He solemnly assured us that the Pretender was riding about the country with "the rogue and vagabond Wesley," disguised as one of his preachers, that they paid no score at the houses of entertainment at which they put up, kept by men of their own kidney, but gave instead promises of the land and property of such of their neighbours as should continue steadfast to King George after the impending invasion. 'Twas a well-known fact, he said, that at their secret sittings the Methodists were sworn, under an awful oath, to take service under the Pretender, to join with the French and Scotch and Irish in saddling a Popish tyrant on free-born Englishmen, and that they met at night for drill in out-of-the-way places among the hills. Sure, if 'tis so well known, we keep our secrets badly from all save ourselves. If Mr. Wesley and his preacher, if any of his preachers ever came to ———, said the foolish young man, 'twould be the duty of true Englishmen to pass them through the horse-pond, to deliver them up to justice, nay, to string them up to the nearest tree. The people here are not easily moved, for the most part, and they do but laugh now at their crazy parson. Nevertheless, in times of disturbance, such teaching might breed mischief among the quietest folk. Teaching, forsooth! 'tis but like the setting on of dogs, which anyone can do who hath wit to shout and hiss and clap his hands.

Tues. 17.—How soon have my words as to the Vicar come true. To-day Mr. Saunders sent me to Farmer Farrant to solicit the settlement of an account, "and," quoth he, "if Robert pays thee, thou canst stay, an' thou wilt, to the preaching in the evening, and bring back the money with thee in the morning. He hath opened his house to the preachers." Now, although Mr. Farrant's farm is not in this parish, some of his men live in it, and have the report of being some of the worst folk therein, drunken, poachers, ever ripe for tumult. They are of those who never go nigh their church, save to be baptized, married, and buried, but having heard of last Sunday's sermon, it had filled them with great delight, and they had sworn to follow the parson's counsel. Mr. Farrant could not pay me the money, which was a providence as things have turned out, as Mr. Saunders, although most pressing for it, must needs own, when I have related to him the circumstances. Notice having been given, a few gathered in the evening in Mr. Farrant's kitchen, to hear the preacher, with whom I had supped. But more remained without, among them those men of his of whom I have spoken, who had got at strong ale as well as hard cider, and made themselves little better than madmen. One of these, with less sense than the horses which 'tis his business to tend, freed from fear of his master by his drunkenness, took upon him to become ringleader of the mob, through which our little congregation had to run the gauntlet, being struck, pelted, and hustled on their way to the place of meeting. When all were inside the shutters were closed, and the door locked and bolted. We had scarce sung the first verse of the hymn when we heard the noise of men coming through the farmyard to the back way, who, beating on the door and windows, loudly demanded that the preacher should be brought out that they might hang him. His parson had bade him hang him, said the ringleader, and if the Pretender and the Pope (for to this the preacher had grown) were not given up at once the house should be pulled down, and we all treated alike. Mr. Farrant, greatly incensed at the fellow's talk, and by the saucy answers which he gave him, would fain have gone out, but was persuaded to remain within by his wife, who, slipping out by another way, let loose the dogs on the mob, and ran across two fields for a justice of the peace. When the justice arrived the dogs were called off, and back came the mob, vowing bloody vengeance, but when they found who had come to our succour, they slunk away muttering, still hanging about the house. Our meeting was no more disturbed, the justice remaining in the house until the end, but taking no part in the service. On leaving he said that, although he would not suffer a pack of low rascals to molest an honest neighbour, he thought Farrant a fool for his pains in bringing them about his doors. When, as we departed, the mob got wind that the justice had left, they again set on us. Shaking myself free from them that had seized me I ran for my life, and, at first, outstripped my pursuers, but, entering a narrow lane, my foot struck against a stone, and I fell prone, my pursuers pouncing upon me. Nevertheless, I was graciously preserved from the fear of man. That comforting scripture was whispered in my ear, "Rejoice not against me, O mine enemy! when I fall, I shall arise." Raising me, the more conveniently to search my pockets—the robbers, for such, 'tis plain, were these rioters, set me against a fence, where they took from me my hat, my watch, and a little loose money which I had about me, but, pressing on me too fiercely, and the wall being of dry stone, they drove it down, and with much clatter we all lay sprawling in the dark. Making no outcry, nay, holding my breath, I rolled out of the reach of mine assailants, and then rising sped my way across the fields, reaching home, praise be to God, unscathed, save for dirt, and a few scratches, and the aforesaid losses. I shall have much to tell my children on the morrow, which little Jack will drink in with greedy ears, although, methinks, he will frown when he heareth that his father was constrained to flee. 'Tis strange the love the little lad hath for tales of highwaymen and fighting. Oh, may the love of God be so shed abroad in his heart by the Holy Ghost given unto him that he may prove the good and faithful soldier of our Lord Jesus Christ!

Wed. 25.—" The Lord is known by the judgment which He executeth : the wicked is snared in the work of his own hand. Higgaion. Selah." The unhappy man who yesterday se'nnight stirred up the baser sort against our brethren, and hath ever since discharged himself from Mr. Farrant's service, and roamed the country from alehouse to alehouse, maddening himself with drink, did again last night gather a mob to disturb the meeting at the farm; but stumbling, as he came on shouting in his fury, he fell with his neck upon a bare scythe, which nigh cut off his head, and so he died in his blood and his sins. "Vengeance is mine, I will repay, saith the Lord."

V.

Fri. May 11.

 THANK the Lord for His goodness in giving me journeying mercies and bringing me back safe to my own home, which He hath kept during my absence under the shadow of His wings. I was greeted on my return with much affection, and not by my little ones alone, but by their mother and my elder children. Now that they see they are not like to starve through my open confession of the Lord Jesus—nay, that, though after so short acquaintance, Mr. Saunders putteth matters of trust into my hands, their old respect for me hath begun to return. O Lord, make them willing to give up all to gain the pearl of great price, and grant that I may not have received seed among thorns! Oh, let not the cares of this world, and the deceitfulness of riches, choke the word so that it become unfruitful!

I have been riding in Glo'stershire and Wilts, collecting

moneys for my master. Mr. Saunders talks as though he would have me believe him in pressing need of cash, forgetting I can discover from the books 'tis no such thing, but that he would have me stern in my demeanour towards his poor debtors, when they plead for time. With the dishonest I must needs be round in my dealing, for I will be no unfaithful steward suffering my master to be defrauded of his due; but when a widow saith unto him, Have patience with me and I will pay thee all, sure, as a Christian man, he should not be so ready to threaten gaol. 'Tis a dead fly that may cause the ointment of his profession to send forth a stinking savour.

At Glo'ster I lay at the Bell, kept by the brother of the famous Mr. George Whitefield, who, 'tis said, was born there. They have a picture of him at the inn, and from it I should judge that the innkeeper favoureth his brother in countenance, save that he hath not his squint. Mrs. Whitefield is a very comely woman. She courteously invited me to take a dish of tea with her, and from her deportment I had hopes that she had cast in her lot with the people of the Lord. But I soon found that, although she had once, moved by the words of the evangelist, her brother-in-law, set out for the Wicket Gate, yet had she, under the influence of her husband, who is but a Worldly-Wiseman, turned aside for the village of Morality; and was very contentedly living therein; being the more secure, inasmuch as, 'tis said, she is a woman of spotless life. Nevertheless, she hath still great reverence for Mr. Whitefield. Our talk turning on Mr. John Wesley, she said that she was sure that he could not be a good man, or Brother George (as she calleth the preacher) would not have broken with him. 'Tis sad that they whose souls were knit together in love like those of Jonathan and David, and who have laboured as brethren to bring our English heathen, as well as them of the Plantations, to a knowledge of the truth, should be sundered. If there be envy, methinks 'tis not in Mr. Wesley's bosom. Mr. Saunders tells me that he would fain be reconciled. Nevertheless, he cannot but look on Mr. Whitefield as an own familiar friend in whom he trusted, but which hath lifted up the heel against him. "For a treacherous wound and for the bewraying of secrets, every friend will depart."

Last Tuesday morning as I stood in the inn yard, one came in and said, "Mr. Wesley hath come suddenly to town, and we have prevailed on him to preach." So I gladly went with the good man, and in a house full of people Mr. Wesley opened unto us that scripture: "Having a form of godliness, but denying the power thereof; from such turn away" (2 Tim. iii. 5). After the service I spake with him, and on reference to my letter, I discovered that he remembered all my circumstances, which is marvellous, considering the number of his correspondents. He told me that he had made mine a case for special prayer, and gave me good hope of the conversion of my wife and children. To have the more of his society, I accompanied him part of the way on his road to Cheltenham, where he was to preach, and again at another place, having already preached at Painswick before he came to Glo'ster.

Sun. 13.—Having heard from Mr. Wesley that on board ship he left off the use of flesh and wine, and confined himself to vegetable food, chiefly rice and biscuit, and that without detriment to the body, and with much edification, I had resolved to begin to-day to essay a like diet; but, in my honour, Sunday now being the only day on which I dine at home, my wife had provided fat ducklings of her own rearing, brought from our old home, staying at home from church to roast them. Now, though she lost nothing in the sermon, nay, rather, 'twas a gain to have escaped it, and the parson maketh but a gabble of the prayers, yet was I sorry when I returned and found that she had tarried for such a purpose. Nevertheless, as she had done it, as she thought, for my pleasure, I knew not what to say, and for the same reason I partook of the ducks. Amity being restored between us, I would not lightly anger her, and doubtless she would have looked upon it as a slight had I refused to taste the dish to which she had given much care for the special humouring of my palate. Nay, the smell being savoury, I fear I needed but little tempting. I must crucify the flesh and the lusts thereof. Sure, at the least, we might always have a cold dinner on the Sabbath. A stir in the kitchen untunes the soul for meditation on divine things. As for the vegetable diet, I will not seek to impose it on my wife, nor on the children, if she urge strong objection, but I will try it for myself. We read of Daniel, Hananiah, Mishael, and Azariah, that they would not eat of the king's meat, or drink of his own wine which he provided, but ate pulse and drank water; nevertheless their countenances appeared fairer and fatter in flesh than all the children which did eat the portion of the king's meat, and at the end of the days there were none like them in knowledge and learning and wisdom.

The evening being so exceeding calm, that even the poplar leaves scarce wagged, I sat in the summer-house for awhile with my little Sue and Jack, and read to them in the *Pilgrim's Progress*, which they must near know by heart, and yet are never weary of hearing read, or spelling out between them. May the Lord make it profitable to their souls, although as yet I fear they love it but as an idle tale of ghosts and giants. Jack would have the fight with Apollyon and Greatheart, but Susan loveth not fighting. This evening I read to her of the green valley of Humiliation beautiful with lilies, and of the boy who sang as he fed his Father's sheep, and had the herb called heart's ease in his breast. O Lord, I thank Thee that Thou hast again given it unto me. We sat out until the flowers closed and the birds, as my little Susan saith, had said their prayers and gone to bed, and, methought, there had not been a happier man in Britain if my beloved ones were but walking in the path that leads to Zion. I poured out my heart in supplication for them at evening worship, and I must wrestle in prayer for them in secret before I retire to rest. 'Tis faith I lack. Oh, could I cry, like him who was called the Prince of God, because he had power with God and had prevailed, "I will not let Thee go, unless Thou bless them!" Lord, teach me how to pray!

Mon. June 11.—'Tis strange that men will make their jest of the Evil One, yea, talk as if the Devil were but the dream of a sick brain, when in our own days, in our very midst, he goeth about as a roaring lion, seeking whom he may devour. To-day, from one who formerly lived in S—— House, until driven from the service by her fears, I have received a particular relation of the noises, apparitions, and other occurrences, doubtless the work of the Powers of Darkness, which have rendered the house next to uninhabitable. The family scarce ever dwell there, but during their absence they are compelled to keep up nigh the full number of servants, for were they not made bold by company, none would stay there; and as things be, notwithstanding the high wages they receive, they are always changing. And, verily, methinks, strong faith in God the Father and our Lord Jesus Christ were needed for any one to tarry in the mansion with untroubled mind. If these accounts be true, 'tis like the Valley of the Shadow of Death; hobgoblins, satyrs, and dragons of the pit, howling and yelling, doleful voices, and the company of fiends.

The A——s of S—— were ever an ungodly and headstrong race, wholly given up to all manner of vice and villany. The present squire is scarce ever at S——, choosing rather to riot in London. But birds of the air betray the secrets of the great; and, verily, of his profligacy could no secret be made. 'Tis too notorious. The A—— of James the First's time, men say, sold his soul to the Evil One, writing the covenant with his own blood, drawn from the back of his left hand, which he had slashed with his dagger for the purpose. All his children born after this unholy deed bore, as it were, the scar of a like gash on their left hands, and it hath come down to their descendants. Thus doth the Lord even now suffer the Beast to put his mark on them that worship him. In the time of the late squire, honest parents trembled for their children, and looked upon the Hall as the castle of a flesh-devouring ogre. And now it seems given up to the demons, as though it were their freehold, to work their will upon, and act their antics. For it is strange how void of purpose appear many of their doings. But God shall yet appear, and His enemies be scattered. The shadows shall flee away. There shall be a new heaven and a new earth,—the holy city, new Jerusalem, coming down from God out of heaven, prepared as a bride adorned for her husband.

Some of the chamber doors at the Hall none can open, strive they never so hard, nor can others ever be shut. As soon as they seem about to close, they fly back with a violence which hath oft levelled those who would have closed them with the ground. Stampings and shoutings have been heard in the dining-hall, but those who entered beheld no man. They saw only the chairs gathered about the dining-table, some tilted on their hind legs, and heard a babble of oaths and drunken laughter, and the calling of ribald toasts. Again, the sound of many feet hath been heard on an upper floor, but they who have gone up have seen no one. They have but heard the feet still beating in measure to the sound of fiddles, and felt the air stirred as by the motion of dancers. Feet pattering up and down the staircases and along the passages have likewise been heard, with screams and giggles. Lights have been blown out, as it were by the rush past of unseen persons, who left a scent upon the air as of the perfume on flying locks; and at times, in still air, as out of mischief, when a light-bearer hath peeped into a dark closet, and found no one therein. On the garret stairs there are plain marks of cloven hoofs, charred, as if stamped by burning feet. The Devil having been seen in form as a satyr, next turned into a rabbit, which was fired at, but, though the shot must have passed clean through it, ran on unharmed. In like manner, men in ancient garb, found wandering about the premises after nightfall, have been shot at and run through with swords, but have gone on their way laughing, while their assailants have been felled and sorely beaten by unseen hands. At times, now here, now there, a smell of brimstone fills the air, and if any of the dogs be present, they whine and sweat, and back to the shelter of the nearest human being, or else putting their tails between their legs, although of the fiercest breeds, they fairly run away, until having reached a safe distance, they lift up their muzzles and howl as if baying the moon. They keep many fierce dogs at the Hall, though surely he were a bold robber who would strive to break in there. Sometimes the Evil One appeareth in the form of a spotted dog, at other times in that of a dun poley bullock, or of a horned, or of a fierce bear which, instead of hair, is covered with dark wool on which the smell of fire hath passed. Sometimes he tempteth in the form of a comely smiling damsel, who, when approached, is turned into a frowning wrinkled witch. One night, the housekeeper entertaining a gossip in her room, with the door locked through timorousness, suddenly the lights burned blue; and looking down they beheld a black cat walking from the door. It walked to the fender, mewed, stretched itself, and lay down upon a footstool, where it tarried for a while, and then arose and walked back to the door, against which it scratched after the manner of cats, until, after having looked back with eyes full of mocking malice (their green, said the housekeeper, seemed to burst into yellow flame), it made a leap at the keyhole, and when the candles burnt clear again, it was gone.

In many of the beds 'tis impossible to have a night's repose. Scarce hath the last stroke of twelve sounded when the bedding begins to heave like a troubled sea, or to buck like an unbroken horse. The curtains are drawn aside with a great rattle of the rings, and the rash man who hath ventured himself into the haunted room seeth a skeleton seated in the chair beside him, or peradventure a corpse, which slowly draws its hand from its mouldering shroud, and lays it, cold as ice, on that of the startled sleeper; or fiendish faces look in upon him in turns from behind the curtains; and if he still persist in remaining, the clothes are drawn from over him, the bed from under him, and finally he is dragged out and buffeted, and, at last, cast violently outside the door. Doubtless, a solemn adjuration in the name of God, uttered by the lips of a man of faith and holiness, might curb these wicked spirits; but 'tis seldom that a godly man finds himself within S—— House. Once only have I heard of their discomfiture by such a man. Their persecution having begun, in mysterious knockings running round the room, as soon as he knelt down to pray, after tarrying for awhile upon his knees, he arose and said, "In the name of the Father, and of the Son, and of the Holy Ghost, I adjure thee by the Living God, that thou depart hence;" and thenceforth throughout that night there was peace. But scarce had the good man departed in the morning, when the devil's knocking began again, with a vigour unusual by daylight, as if in exultation at being rid of his presence. Most terrible, however, are the clanking of chains, the groaning, the moaning, and the shrieks of torment which are heard issuing, as it were, from the bowels of the earth, in the darkness of the night. Some say there is at S—— a book in which, on the death of each squire, an unseen hand, with an unseen pen, inscribes his name, in characters which singe the paper, and that the blots the pen maketh are of molten metal or boiling blood. But this seems to me an idle tale. Sure, the truth is sufficient dreadful.

VI.

Mon. Sept. 3.

THIS day we have bound our Patty to Mrs. Spaull, the milliner and mantua-maker, in the Abbey Churchyard. I have laid the case before the Lord, but at times I fear that I have been too ready to take my wife's likings for the Spirit's leadings. The arrangement will be to our easement and the temporal advantage of the child, inasmuch as she will not only receive board and lodging and her clothes, but likewise a wage from the beginning of her second year of service, and Mistress Spaull is well able to teach her the trade, and afterwards advance her in the world—none better. My wife says 'twill be the making of the girl. God grant it prove not her undoing. She hath good looks, and is vain of them, and I fear her poor mother, dearly, doubtless, though she love her, hath fostered her folly. 'Tis true that " Beauty is but skin deep," " Handsome is that handsome does," and such-like sayings, are ever on my wife's lips; but 'tis plain that she maketh a show of undervaluing good looks, because she takes as certain that all allow them to her. 'Tis scarce becoming in a woman of her age to bridle as she doth when folk say that they can see nothing of the father in Patty, that she is her own mother's child. Though, indeed, 'tis rather what her mother was, than what she is, that Patty calls to mind; and, to say truth, my little Jack, who is said most to feature me, is in my eyes, in his way, as well-favoured as any of my children. 'Tis strange the price which persons, otherwise of sense, put upon their faces, which a week's small-pox can turn to hideous masks. If a woman hath once been handsome she never forgets it, but to her dying day thinketh she is so still; and, verily, many born ugly are guilty of like folly. 'Tis true that Mistress Spaull hath promised to look after my child, and is reputed to be a motherly, and upright, as well as notable woman. But her thoughts are not as my thoughts, her ways as my ways, in these matters. And, moreover, there will be young fellow-workers to lead my child astray. I misdoubt me whether I have done that which is pleasing in the sight of God, in thrusting her into the thick of the fire of folly with a heart untouched by grace. Even had she been built up in the faith 'twould have been a sore trial for her. My spirit is stirred within me when I see how the city is almost wholly given up unto frivolity. What a poor creature at bottom is this overbearing King of Bath, on whose words men hang as on Herod's, as though not a man but a god had spoken. What will his laced coat and his white hat, his gilt coach and six grey horses, his running footmen, his outriders, and his trumpeters profit him at the last great day? Nay, what is he now but one fool to whom a crowd of bigger fools bow down? Doth not the Lord call him a fool that had made up his mind to take his ease, eat, drink, and be merry, forgetting that his soul would be required of him? "What shall it profit a man, if he shall gain the whole world, and lose his own soul?"

Mr. Saunders tells that a while since this great man was put to silence by an old woman. He had been speaking great swelling words of what he would do if Mr. John Wesley came to preach in his kingdom, and a great congregation had assembled to witness their meeting, most expecting that the quiet little clergyman would be utterly confounded by the blustering beau. Presently in he came swaggering and speaking words of folly; and when Mr. Wesley had exposed his ignorance of law and logic, still persisted in his demand to know why the Methodists had come together. Thereupon, from the poorer part of the congregation, there arose a voice, "Sir, leave him to me, let an old woman answer him. You, Mr. Nash, take care of your body; we take care of our souls; and for the food of our souls are we come here." And, answering her never a word, the great man slunk away. 'Tis easy to picture the perturbation among the silversmiths of pleasure when news got abroad that their Diana had been preached against, their Demetrius openly defied and discomfited. The young bloods buzzed about like angry wasps, exclaiming " Which is he?" " Where is he?" as if minded, in spite of the cloth, to plunge their swords into the troubler of their peace. But when Mr. Wesley quietly answered, " I am he," they looked sheepish and held their tongues.

Sat. 8.—Before going to business this morning, I went to the Churchyard to see my daughter, and to say that, with her mistress's permission, I would call for her in the evening to convey her to her home to spend the Sabbath with us, promising that she should be back to her work betimes on Monday. I had purposed that it should so be settled when she was bound, but through oversight omitted to state my wish. To my sorrow Mistress Spaull raised objection, at which, to my greater sorrow, Martha manifested pleasure. Mistress Spaull hath promised that she shall attend the Abbey services twice in the day, and doubtless she will hear better sermons there than from our vicar, but all her day will not be spent at the Abbey nor in the house. I would fain have had her under her mother's eye. Even at the Abbey, moreover, I fear that she may fall in with bad example. In the week there is service twice a day, to which some of the fine ladies and gentlemen go much as to the Pump-room or the Assembly, and from what I witness, behave therein with as little reverence. I saw gentlewomen in their bathing-clothes carried in chairs to the baths, into which I have been told they descend to the sound of music, and when the attendants have placed their nosegays, their snuff-boxes, and handkerchiefs on floating trays, the gentlemen leaning over from the gallery, pay them compliments upon their beauty. Methinks 'tis not a seemly spectacle in a Christian land. Some, verily, have no beauty left to be complimented on. I would that Patty could read the lesson writ in the face of the old Lady D——, a famous beauty in her day, but now 'tis a death's head covered with parchment, and she must put rouge upon the parchment. Not a tooth, and scarce a hair of her own hath she left, and yet is she as proud of her train of followers, who do but mock her, as if she was not seventy, but seventeen. Of those I saw taking the waters how many, I marvel, did it for their health's sake, how many for mere fashion. Truly, if we may judge from their grimaces, they pay a heavy tax for their modishness, offer liberal sacrifice to their divinity. In the coffee-rooms sat the gentlemen, sipping their coffee, and tea, and chocolate, munching their buns and buttered rolls; and in the toy-shops the ladies reading the news and cheapening trinkets. And how would the day thus begun be finished? In public breakfasts, in concerts public and private, in idle rambles and rides along the London Road and over the Downs with no purpose but to sharpen the appetite for their mutton, in empty visits and tea-drinkings at the Rooms, in dances and card-parties, with loss of time, temper, cash, and character, in going indifferently to the Playhouse or to prayers! Is this, avoiding mention of grosser iniquities, shamelessly practised, a life for a mere rational being? How oft would the pagan who exclaimed, " I have lost a day," at the end of one on which he had done no good deed, have to repeat his exclamation, did he live with and as our Bath heathen? But for men who should know that they have immortal souls, which must be saved by the precious blood of Christ, or else ever-lastingly perish, 'tis stark, staring madness. We read that we "know perfectly that the day of the Lord so cometh as a thief in the night." Did we but know it with a feeling knowledge! What if to-night the trumpet should sound, the stars fall from heaven like untimely figs, the grave and the sea give up their dead, the heavens be rolled together as a scroll, the heaven and earth flee away, and all the dead, small and great, be called to stand before God, to be judged by their works, and faith, out of the things written in the opened books! Nay, what if the internal fire which, the learned say, heateth the waters in which the fribbles of Bath complacently soak themselves, giving and taking compliments, were to force its way to the surface, and convert our green valley into a lake of burning brimstone!

Sun. 9.—This hath been a calm and sunny day, and yet a shadow seemed to rest upon our house. So far as I remember, 'tis the first Sabbath a child of ours hath spent away from home. Her mother, like myself, had thought that we should have had Patty with us once a week, and purposes journeying into Bath upon the morrow to speak with Mistress Spaull upon the matter. O Lord, watch over my dear child. Leave her not in temptation. Have mercy upon her, and incline her heart to keep thy laws.

Mon. 10.—My wife's journey hath been in vain. Mistress Spaull saith 'twould breed jealousy, and disorder her household, were she to suffer Patty to visit us every week. Now and again, she saith, she may come, and promises to look well after her. Indeed, she was somewhat short with my wife for seeming to doubt of her care, saying that she had no need to go begging for 'prentices, and that we were full welcome to have the girl home for good, an we chose. Thereupon, my wife put the blame upon me. I would that I may never feel myself more to blame in this matter, but my heart misgiveth.

VII.

Mon. Oct. 29.

 FRIEND of my master's, who hath been travelling in Cornwall, gave us a long narrative of the persecution which the Methodists have there been called upon to endure. When they assemble, the mob threaten to break open the doors, and knock down the brethren like bought bullocks. Chiefly, however, do they thirst after the preachers' blood. Without that, they say, they never will be satisfied. At Camborne, one of the preachers, while preaching, was pulled down by a big bully and haled out to the mob, who, after keeping him prisoner from the Sunday until the Tuesday, then carried him before the Penzance Justices, by whom, in defiance of law and reason, he was committed to Bodmin gaol. The two or three who have joined themselves to me here have not yet been molested; but 'tis told me that our meetings, quiet though they be, have enraged the Vicar,

who sweareth that, if he cannot otherwise drive me from the village, he will have me pressed for a soldier. The laws are now so strained if 'tis a Methodist that must be got rid of, that 'tis hard to say what may or may not be done against us, but sure this is scarce possible. Lord, I am in thy hands.

Mon. Nov. 5.—Mischief is brewing. My little Jack having run out to see the fireworks was seized by rough lads, who threatened to fling him into the bonfire for a "little Papish." But "Nay, nay," said a man, delivering him out of their hands, "'tis the old cock, not the cockerel, we must roast." It was pretty to see the little Susan's love for her brother when he ran in and told the story. The tears came to her eyes, her face flushed angry red, and, though of a most gentle disposition, she clenched her little fists, which could scarce harm a fly. Then flinging her arms round Jack she burst into a flood of weeping, as she nigh smothered him with kisses, and all the evening after never suffered him out of her sight until he went to bed. Nay, her mother tells me that she found her creeping from her own room in her nightgown to see that her brother was safe in his crib. She ——

Tues. 6.—Last night I was interrupted in my writing. The drunken mob had kicked a tar barrel against my wood stack, which soon kindled, and when I went out to beat down the flames I was driven back with burning brands. My poor wife was treated in like fashion, and the few friends who came to our help. All the while the Vicar was looking on, not abetting, indeed, but he did nothing to restrain until my stack was consumed. Then he bade the mob go away, which, after a time, they did, swearing that next time it should be the house. Some of them whom I have seen to-day, being sobered, are ashamed of their last night's doings, but put the blame on the free drink given, they say, by the Vicar's order. Thanks to his zeal against the Pope, we, who bear him as little love, spent a most anxious night, scarce one, after our scare, getting a wink of sleep.

Wed. 7.—During my absence the Vicar visited my wife, and professed great sorrow for the destruction of my property. And more, he promised that he would keep me in wood throughout the winter, if she would prevail upon me to discontinue my meetings with the brethren. He would fain, he said, have hindered the mob, but knew 'twas no use speaking unto drunken men, especially when, in a way, their wrath was righteous, inasmuch as I had proved myself disloyal to my Church and King. He thought to wheedle her by saying how much he pitied her misfortune in being exposed to such attacks, through no fault of hers, but because her husband was a Methodist. He found soon that he was smoothing a thistle. My poor wife hath little love for

Methodists, but even worse she hates a lying tongue; and so she spake up bravely. "Who made the men drunken, your Reverence?" she said. "They went at your bidding, and they came. My husband is a better Englishman than you." Peradventure, there was no great praise in that last saying, but it cheered my heart to find that she had still so much of her old love left for me. O Lord, let not the ties of affection prove a snare unto me. As she related all this, I felt, for the time, as if I could, to give her pleasure in return, have promised to discontinue our meetings. Thanks be to Thee, O Lord, these words were then whispered in my ears, " Every one that hath forsaken houses, or brethren, or sisters, or father, or mother, or wife, or children, or lands, for my name's sake, shall receive an hundredfold, and shall inherit everlasting life." Nevertheless, that is an hard saying. For no earthly reward, methinks, could I in very deed *forsake* my wife and children, and for the next world, sure for their salvation, if so it could be brought about, a man ought to be willing to become a castaway. 'Tis strange, too, that the verse beginneth with "houses" and ends with "lands," as if those were the possessions most hard to part with. I know not, having neither; but the verse should teach us not to be harsh in our judgment on the covetousness of those who have. He who made us must know how we are made.

Thurs. 8.—This day the rider of a merchant, with whom Mr. Saunders doth business, pressed me to dine with him at the ordinary. I know not why, save that I had spoilt his bargain with my master. 'Twas one from which Mr. Saunders would have gotten gain, and he appeared ready to strike; but feeling that by so doing he would have risked his character for godliness, and, far worse, have given worldly men good excuse for scoffing at those who make profession of being ruled by a higher law, in whatsoever they do, than are they who sit still in darkness, I openly spake my mind. Mr. Saunders said nothing, but it was plain to see that he was much displeased. The rider, on the other hand, laughing, swore he bore no malice, but must carry me off to dinner. I rebuked him for his profanity, but he still insisted on my company, and not being able to find excuse, without the giving of unnecessary offence, I went with him. Perchance he thought to wheedle me by his show of hospitality, and then, plying me with wine, to make of me a nose of wax for his purpose. Perhaps 'twas mere good nature. I cannot say. Having come into the room at the inn, and finding that the company were about to fall to like heathens, I craved leave to ask a blessing. They stared and smiled, but made no objection. Neither did they mock, save one, that thought himself a wag, who must say Amen after me very loud, and through his nose, but none laughed; and the maid, who waited upon us, being allowed, owing to her comeliness, to indulge herself in freedoms with the customers of the house, bade him be silent for a silly jackanapes. The rider said no more about the bargain, and before we parted I found opportunity to speak to him with much plainness, which he took in good part, shaking me heartily by the hand. Mr. Saunders was very stiff with me when I returned to business, but I must serve God rather than man.

Sat. 10.—O Lord, Thou hast brought me unto the end of another week. With most humble and grateful heart would I desire to thank Thee for Thy goodness unto me therein. It hath been a week of trials and mercies.

The market of Bath being famous for its milk, butter, fruit, and vegetables, and fowls, mutton, and all manner of food being good and plenty in the city, skilled cooks have likewise been bred there, and Bath cookmaids are in great request. To-day, Mrs. Spaull sent word that she would speak with me, and when I went to her shop, advised me that one of her customers, a lady of quality, having asked her to find her a cookmaid, she had named our Hester, having heard from Patty that she was skilled in kitchen work; and so, indeed, are all the girls, according to their ages, their mother, who is second to none in such matters, training them most carefully. Mistress Spaull having named the wages, most liberal, bade me make up my mind at once, but I said that I must have time for consideration. "Well," she saith, "take the offer home and sleep upon it, sleep twice upon it, and bring your answer on Monday. I must be ready with mine then. . My lady cannot be kept waiting. Most folk would have jumped at the place." When I came home and told my wife and Hester, they were both eager that I should close with the lady, Hester, as being the elder, feeling huffed that Patty should have gone out into the world before her. But my heart hath so oft been troubled since I suffered myself to be persuaded to place that dear child with Mistress Spaull that I was resolved not to part with another child, except under the manifest guidance of Providence. Accordingly I entered into my closet, and laid the case before the Lord, praying Him to make my way clear before me. Then, still upon my knees, I opened my Bible, and read, "Count not thine handmaid for a daughter of Belial."

'Twas a manifest warning, and going out I announced my resolve to send my thanks to the lady, but to refuse her offer. I have since had nothing but sulky looks from Hester, and, though she saith nothing, my wife is plainly angered. But what other could I do? 'Twould have been courting judgment on my daughter and myself to run counter to so plain a declaration of the will of God.

Dear Patty was loving when I spake with her to-day, but it grieved me to see her already clad in gay worldly attire. O Lord, bring her unto Thee, make her Thy meek and lowly child. "Whose adorning let it not be that outward adorning of plaiting the hair, and of wearing of gold, or of putting on of apparel; but let it be the hidden man of the heart, in that which is not corruptible, even the ornament of a meek and quiet spirit, which is in the sight of God of great price. For after this manner in the old time the holy women also, who trusted in God, adorned themselves."

Mon. 12.—When I told Mistress Spauil this morning, whilst giving her thanks for her kindness, that I had resolved to keep Hester still with us, she fair called me a fool for my pains. She had but to let it be known that she had such a place in her gift, and scores of girls would come buzzing about her shop, like flies about a honey-pot. I had had the refusal of it, she said, flying into a rage, but she would never give me another such chance. I need never again come begging to her about my children. She washed her hands of all of them, except Patty. 'Twas lucky she had more wit than her father; and more of the same purport, and with scant courtesy Sure, 'twas not I that wished to 'prentice the dear child

VIII.

Wed. Nov. 14.

ESTERDAY, in the evening, Mr. Wesley arrived in Bath, but, being pressed for time, was constrained to excuse himself from his promise of coming to ——. I stayed late in the city, that I might enjoy the privilege of his conversation. He told us of his life in the Plantations. There, too, it seems, he was taken for a Papist, or near akin to one, owing to the strictness of his life, which, sure, was a satire on the Protestants who made the objection. The negroes, he saith, drank in the word as a thirsty land drinketh in the rain. Of the Indians, for the most part, he hath but little hope, unless Christian men will, so to speak, storm the Throne of Grace on their behalf. They are dead in trespasses and sins, and yet wise in their own eyes. The land, it seems, is not all fat and fertile, as some have represented. There is much sand and marsh. When a town hath been laid out, the streets not built upon are used for corn fields. In his journeyings he oft risked his life, and underwent many hardships from heat and weariness, cold and hunger. The Indian potato, Mr. Wesley saith, is very sweet, and bigger than ours, and melons grow to a great size in the open air, yielding from their moist red flesh, which melts in the mouth, a most refreshing drink. He was grieved at not being able to come to ——, more especially as he had given his word that he would do so, but 'twas plainly impossible. When I asked him to promise that he would come the next time he visited these parts, "Nay, brother," said he, "I will make no more absolute promises, but come if the Lord be willing." He inquired after my dear wife and children, and encouraged me still to go on praying on their behalf. "Nothing doubting, brother, nothing doubting," he said, twice over.

Thur. 15.—Yesterday, Mr. Wesley's words still cheered me; but as I walked home this evening my heart sank within me when I thought of my wife and children still unconverted, and of the very few others in this place whom I have been instrumental in bringing to a knowledge of the truth. We are still, in very fact, but two or three. Scarcely, however, had I eaten my supper, when one came, begging me to go at once to John Shaw's, who was very ill, and wanted to see me. I had known that the old man was fast failing, and had more than once called to speak with him, but he refused to listen to me. In his youth and manhood he followed the sea, and gave himself up to unbridled licentiousness. Deplorably common though the use of profane language at present is, his oaths were of so specially frightful a kind that they made the blood run cold. He was a sinner against light. He was not ignorant of the plan of salvation, but worked the very words of Scripture into horrible blasphemy. But now the sorrows of death compassed him, the pains of hell had gotten hold upon him. When I went into his room, I found him in an agony of terror. In vain at first did I point out that there was mercy for the vilest sinner, that the thief had been pardoned on the very cross. He shook his head and moaned: "I also will laugh at your calamity; I will mock when your fear cometh; when your fear cometh as desolation, and your destruction cometh as a whirlwind."

"Ay, pray, pray, pray," he cried, when I knelt down beside his bed, "but 'tis no use, no good, too late, too late!" Nevertheless, I continued instant in prayer for more than two hours. When my bodily strength failed me, I prayed silently until I had recovered my voice. A little before eleven his breathing, which had been very laboured, became easier, and he murmured something gently. I rose and put my ears to his lips. "I can, I do believe that Christ hath saved me," he said, faintly. As he seemed to be gasping for breath, I raised him in my arms. As I did so, although the room was lighted by one long-wicked candle only, I could see his face brightening with an unearthly radiance as though the spirit of prophecy had come upon him. In a firmer voice he said, "And other folk in this place shall be saved. Tell them, when I am gone, that I was saved by Jesu's blood, and He who saved wicked old Jack Shaw can save anybody." When I laid him back on his pillow, he was dead.

Sun. 18.—John Shaw was buried between services. There was a great gathering, word having been spread abroad that he had left a message for me to deliver. The Vicar had heard of it, and forbade me to disturb the service. "Sir, I have no intention," I replied, but he was not satisfied. With language most unseemly for such a time and place, he accused me of I know not what. Some of the crowd calling upon me to speak out, he threatened to indict me for riot in a churchyard, but, save to say to the crowd, "Not now," I held my peace, and he, seeing that the crowd turned angry looks upon him, went on with the service. When it was over, I went out, the crowd following quietly, and taking my stand under the great tree outside the churchyard gate, from which the leaves fell fast, as though to mind us that we all do fade in like fashion, I related the circumstances of John Shaw's death, and delivered his message, afterwards proceeding to exhort my hearers to come to Christ at once. The Vicar bade me hold my peace, and when I still spake on, strove to come at me in his rage, but was hindered by the crowd; whereupon he turned and went away in a rage, with many threats of the punishment in store for all of us. Soon after was heard the blowing of two cow-horns, one by the parson's man inside the stable-gates, and the other by the drunken, half-witted fellow, Sam Maw, but his having been taken from him, the parson's man soon, for very shame, desisted. I spoke for nigh an hour with a freedom of speech and boldness of heart which would have astonished me, had I not called to mind that what I said had been given unto me to say. "Whatsoever shall be given you in that hour, that speak ye; for it is not ye that speak, but the Holy Ghost." Throughout I was listened to with deep attention. God grant that the seed thus sown may bring forth fruit an hundred fold.

Sun. Dec. 2.—John Shaw's word is fulfilled. During the past week there hath been a most gracious outpouring of the Spirit in this place. "This is the Lord's doing; it is marvellous in our eyes. This is the day which the Lord hath made; we will rejoice and be glad in it." I have not till now had leisure to write in my journals. Far into the watches of the night our meetings have been kept up, and, glory be to God, many have found peace; some who, like John Shaw, had drunk iniquity like water. Their hearts of stone have been smitten; they have cried aloud for mercy with exceeding loud and bitter cries. The Spirit hath helped their infirmities, for when they knew not what they should pray for as they ought, the Spirit itself made intercession for them with groanings which cannot be uttered. One of the Moravian Brethren in Bath, to whom with thankfulness I related the great things which God had done for our parish, professed himself greatly scandalized at what he named our tumult. "My doctrine shall drop as the rain," he quoted; "my speech shall distil as the dew, as the small rain upon the tender herb, and as the showers upon the grass." "But the Lord was not in the wind; and after the wind an earthquake, but the Lord was not in the earthquake; and after the earthquake a fire, but the Lord was not in the fire; and after the fire, a still small voice."

But sure, we are bidden to cry aloud, and spare not, —"Awake, thou that sleepest; arise from the dead, and Christ shall give thee light." And when the foundations of the prison were shaken, and the jailer sprang in, and came trembling, and fell down before Paul and Silas, methinks 'twas not in a whisper that he asked, "Sirs, what must I do to be saved?"

Verily, now do I see that the Lord's hand is not shortened that it cannot save; neither His ear heavy that it cannot hear. I had looked upon this village as a valley of dry bones, and had nigh doubted within my heart whether they could ever live, for lo! they were very dry. But the dry bones have heard the word of the Lord, breath hath entered into them, and now they live. What marvel that there hath been a noise and a shaking? We have met together for intercession and praise, as the work hath run from house to house like fire; like fire again leaving some untouched, but leaping on to a farther dwelling at a bound.

There have been many marvellous manifestations of the Lord's power, mighty to save. The maid at the *Blue Boar* was suddenly seized, and became as one mad. But when I bade her look to Christ, as the Israelites looked to the brazen serpent lifted up in the wilderness, in an instant she obtained mercy. The storm ceased, and there was a great calm. Her mistress hath discharged her without warning, but this will be to the profit of her soul.

The little lad Pyke is another monument of saving grace. From his birth he hath been a great cross to his parents, especially his poor mother; now seeming wanting in his intellects, and again as though he were bewitched or possessed of a devil, or a changeling, so full was he of malice and wanton mischief. He had oft-times fallen into the fire, and oft into the water. He swallowed pins and needles, afterwards drawing them forth from sundry parts of his body, and would worry his own and others' flesh as a dog mumbles a sheep's foot, making deep and bloody wounds, and leaving the marks of his teeth for months. At other times he would strip, tear his clothes to tatters, or cast them into the fire, and rush stark naked through the village. At the commencement of the work of grace here he became even more than ordinarily violent and wilful, but, his mother having sent for me, I went and prayed over him, and, to all appearance, the child has been cured from that very hour.

As I was speaking on, "Thou, Lord, which knowest the hearts of all," Agnes ———, who had ever before had the repute of a virtuous and modest maiden, suddenly stood up in the midst of the congregation and, with many tears, made open confession of secret iniquity. We encouraged her to cast herself at the foot of the cross, relying only on the precious blood of the Lord Jesus Christ; and He who hath said, "Though your sins be as scarlet, they shall be as white as snow; though they be red like crimson, they shall be as wool," graciously spake peace to her soul.

James Somerton, the quarryman, came in and disturbed our meeting, affirming that we were all hypocrites.

But that night I was awakened out of sleep. James stood below, declaring that he had discovered that he had spoken at the prompting of the devil, and that sore pricked by his conscience, he had risen from his bed, and wandered about in the cold and dark for nearly three hours. I went down and let him into the kitchen, where, having blown up the dying fire, and put on fresh fuel, I prayed with him until God in like manner kindled faith in his cold black heart, and having received the Spirit of adoption, he was enabled to cry Abba, Father. The next night Nicholas Sayers, the blacksmith's man, who likewise had come to our meeting to mock, was making sport of three young women who had fallen, crying, to the ground, under deep conviction of sin, when suddenly the strong man dropped to the ground as though he had been shot; immediately thereafter wallowing, writhing, and tossing as though rent by a devil. 'Twas as much as many men could contrive to prevent him from doing himself a mischief. Meanwhile his outcries were terrible. His bones waxed old through his roaring, and many hearts melted at the sound thereof. Two more men were pricked to the heart, and fell upon their knees loudly imploring mercy. We continued in prayer with them, and before midnight God gave rest to their souls, but 'twas nigh upon one before Nicholas found peace.

Some came from the next parish to our meeting, laughing and saying that their Squire and Parson had sent them to us to be converted, and that we must be quick about it, as their road home was bad to travel without a moon. But their jesting ceased, and deep seriousness came upon them as I reasoned with them of righteousness, temperance, and judgment to come. Alas! however, like Felix, they put off acting on their conviction until a more convenient season. Nevertheless, they left our meeting far more orderly than they had entered it, saying, as they departed, that they would trouble us no more.

At times our whole assembly has been stirred as by a rushing mighty wind filling the whole house, but when we have hoped that the day of Pentecost had fully come, we have been disappointed to find that these seasons of general moving were not so fruitful in conversions as times in which now one and another afterwards was separately seized, and could be prayed for singly.

Sarah Kinns's was a noteworthy case. Her father, an ignorant man, calling us in profane scorn "the Holy Ghosters," finding that Sarah talked much about her sins, and from having been a merry maid was ever moping, went to the Vicar and asked his counsel. That poor blind leader of the blind, Kinns boasted, answered that 'twas mere megrims troubled his daughter, and that what she wanted was a doctor or a wake. "If the lads would get well drunken, and the lasses all pick sweethearts," Kinns affirms the parson to have said, "we should hear no more of your Methodists." The foolish man, Kinns, did, accordingly, take his daughter to Frome fair, where he drank abundance of the strong ale for which that town is too famous (I was told when I passed through it that there is at one of its inns a huge cask containing many hogsheads), and took his pleasure after his swinish manner. But though he would have her dance in the booths, and bought her fairings of the pedlery, Sarah continued of a sorrowful spirit. Nay, she was worse when she came back than when she started. During the father's absence the mother invited me to visit her child. I found her sitting motionless, her eyes, around which were great black rings, fixed upon the ground. Suddenly her lips twitched, her countenance was distorted, and she shrieked aloud, her limbs being tossed about wildly meanwhile, as though not of her own will, but moved by some unseen power that had taken possession of her.

"It is too late," she cried, like old John Shaw. "I might have been saved if father had not taken me to Frome; but now I am damned. I cannot be saved; I won't be saved. Come, take me, Devil, dear Devil, just as I am, with all my sins. Yea, come quickly, O Lord

Devil," and at this she cast herself upon the ground, and, putting her hands together, bowed her head as if in worship, still muttering, " O Lord Devil," so that her mother ran out in fright. And, indeed, 'twas very dreadful to be brought thus face to face with the Prince of Darkness triumphing over the soul he had ensnared. To drown the more and more awful blasphemies which she uttered, I started a hymn, but at every mention of the name of Christ she screamed so frightfully, and was racked by such hideous tortures, that I was constrained to desist. So, falling on my knees, and stopping my ears, so that I might not hear her wicked words, I prayed without ceasing, until, at last, she fell asleep. After about an hour, during which I had still knelt beside her praying, she woke calmed, and in her right mind. With a sweet smile upon her lips, she said, " I have been with the Devil, but Christ descended into hell, and led me out. Glory for ever to His name !"

Jane Lycet's experience, likewise, was remarkable. After attending one of our prayer-meetings, she fell, on her return home, into a trance, in which she continued for twenty-four hours. One of our sisters, trusting to deepen the impression which Jane had received at the meeting, accompanied her home, and had just uttered those blessed words, which may be named the Gospel in a nut-shell, " Believe in the Lord Jesus Christ, and thou shalt be saved," when, as before said, Jane became insensible. In a short time she turned key-cold. A mirror placed over her mouth was not dimmed, nor was a feather stirred. No pulse, no beating of the heart, could be discovered. The doctors who attended her gave her up for dead, and her friends were preparing to lay her out, when she came to herself, saying, "Lord, I believe. Help Thou my unbelief." And then she related the vision she had seen. She had, she said, been to Burslem, in Staffordshire, from which she came, but which she had not visited since she was a child; and, finding all her kinsfolk dead or gone, and that she had faded from the recollection of their acquaintance, she had been guided by one who said, "I will never leave thee nor forsake thee," to Newcastle-under-Lyne, and, entering into the house of a hatter, was greeted by him as his niece. Then she called to mind that she had an uncle there, her mother's favourite brother, who had made much of her when a child, and between whom and her letters had passed, though but rarely, since she took up her abode at ———. Her uncle told her that he had been brought to a knowledge of the truth by a word in season, spoken to him by Mr. Wesley, when passing through the town in '38. He begged her to kneel down with him, and prayed that she might be a partaker of the like blessed experience, and she believed that she was still at Newcastle, rising from her knees, when she uttered the words which I have cited. A while after came a messenger, announcing that her uncle at Newcastle had died at the very time in which she had recovered from her trance, that he had left her all his substance, and that his last hours had been spent in praying for her salvation.

With another record of the authority which the Evil One is for a time allowed to exercise over the mind, soul, and body of those whom the Spirit hath elected to be heirs of salvation, I will conclude for the present my narrative of the wonderful work recently wrought in this parish.

Keziah Elworthy, a young woman convinced of sin, having sent for me to pray with her, when I went in she burst into a fit of horrid mocking laughter, such as might ring in hell, spat upon me, nay, I thought she would have buffeted me. In a voice that was not her own she cried, " Ha, ha! What can you do? She is mine. Begone." " Nay, stay," she added feebly, in her own voice, but again in the other there was thundered out, " Begone. Say ' Begone ' I bid thee, or thy torment shall be greater." And in her own voice, though with a quavering scornfulness, she exclaimed, " Begone. I sent not for thee, or, if I did, 'twas but to mock thee." The hair of my flesh stood up. 'Twas plain that one had entered into her who strove to obtain full mastery over her still, though feebly, struggling will.

"Oh, neighbour Pidgeon," she suddenly exclaimed, but instantly she was thrown upon the floor, and grievously tormented; her screams of anguish confused with the mocking laughter of the fiend, and words of foulest blasphemy uttered in her own faltering voice.

"I adjure thee that thou torment her not," I cried, in an agony of dread and pity.

At that she leaped upon me, the fiend within her answering, "Jesus I know, and Paul I know, but who art thou?" Doubtless he had prevailed against me, and 1 should have fled from the house naked and wounded. if even I had been suffered to escape with my life, had I not fallen on my knees and prayed to the Father, for the sake of Him who cast out devils, to give me the mastery in this dire conflict. I felt the Heaven-sent virtue pouring into me. I thrilled all over as it rushed like a loosened water-course through my throbbing frame, and rising to my feet, I exclaimed, "In the name of the Holy Trinity I adjure thee that thou no more torment her. Come out of her, thou unclean spirit, and enter no more into her!" And the spirit cried, and rent her sore, but he came out of her, leaving her as one dead. Friends coming in, we prayed over her and she revived, and is now rejoicing in the full assurance of hope unto the end.

Thus, in the comparative leisure of this day have I related some of the wonderful works of God in this place. I humbly thank thee, O Father, for having made me Thy instrument, in however small degree, in bringing my neighbours unto Thee. O Lord, let me not be puffed up, and sacrifice unto my own net, and burn incense unto my drag. But, sure, 'twould be impossible after my late experience of my impotence and Thine almighty power. "Behold even to the moon, and it shineth not; yea, the stars are not pure in His sight. How much less man that is a worm?" What am I but a worm, yea, less than a worm, in Thy sight, O Lord God of Hosts? "With Thine own right hand, and Thy holy arm, hast Thou gotten Thyself the victory."

IX.

Sat. Dec. 15.

FOR a time the work is stayed, but, thanks be to God, those who have been called walk worthy of the Lord unto all pleasing, being fruitful in every good work and increasing in the knowledge of God, strengthened with all might, according to His glorious power, unto all patience and long-suffering with joyfulness; giving thanks unto the Father, which hath made them meet to be partakers of the inheritance of the saints in light; who hath delivered them from the power of darkness, and hath translated us into the kingdom of His dear Son. Nevertheless, although 'tis great cause for thankfulness that here where the people sat in darkness there hath arisen a great light, 'tis still the many that be called, the few chosen. How many of my neighbours are still unregenerate! And, alas, it cuts me to the heart that while the dew of the Spirit hath dropped plenteously around, my own fleece hath continued dry. Not one of my family hath been touched. Nay, my poor wife's old angry hatred of the Methodists hath been revived and strengthened. She fears that my zeal for the Gospel may again hinder my worldly advancement; and, indeed, Mr. Saunders hath shown no great rejoicing over the work of the Spirit in our midst, although he cannot lay to my charge that I have neglected his business. Methinks that, as a professor, he might have somewhat abridged my hours of secular business to give me fuller opportunity to labour for the Lord. But he hath not, and I will not judge him. To his own master he shall stand or fall. But I may here say that the opposition of my wife and the coldness of my family are a cross unto me, inasmuch as they may prove a stumbling-block in the way of sinners who might otherwise come within hearing of the Gospel. The sons of Belial make a scoff of my powerlessness to move my kindred. "The zaint," say they, "is too well knowan at huome. Let un convart his own volk avore he talk to uz."

Mon. 17.—As I came in from Bath I heard the beating of a drum, and, passing the *Blue Boar*, I saw the zany they call Merry Andrew beating the drum in the gate-way of the yard. A puppet-show man had set up his stage within, and a crowded company had assembled to witness the absurd, nay more, immoral performance, for 'twas a profane stage-play the figures acted. In the crowd were many children, among them my little Susan and Jack, and, when I called to them to come out, those who should have known better would have prevented them, until Sue began to weep, whereupon Jacky forced a way for her. But when nigh breathless he had brought out his sister, he likewise appeared inclined to weep at having been interrupted in what, alas! he had thought an entertainment. I take it not kindly that my wife should have suffered the children to go to such a place, knowing, as she doth, my aversion to these graven images of fools which others show to the delight of more.

Wed. 19.—Mr. Saunders having attended Chippenham Fair last week, I was sent to complain of the rustiness and short weight of the bacon sent in the stead of that which, he saith, he bought, and to demand restitution; but in this I failed. " Nay, nay," said the seller, "'tis the same, to an ounce weight, that thy master bought. They say 'tis as hard to take thy master at unawares as to catch a weasel napping; that when he sleeps, he still hath one eye open like the Bristol folk. What could he expect at the price to which he beat me down? Tut, tut, 'twill be no loss, I warrant. I know him well. You'll sell it between you at good profit as best Wiltshire." 'Tis grievous to hear these things said of one who, save for his shortcomings caused by love of filthy lucre, is, I believe, God's servant. 'Tis hard, too, to be taken for his abettor in these doubtful, if they be not downright dishonest practices. Having heard that to-morrow there will be a more than ordinary show of cheese at Chipping Sodbury Market, he hath set out over-night to buy there. I hope he will make no more such bargains. They cause great grief to his good wife, who is an Israelite indeed, in whom there is no guile. Having invited me to take tea with her this evening, she related to me how three years ago Mr. Wesley formed the Bath Society; persuading a few, who before had been content to come to Jesus secretly, for fear of the gay gentry and them which depend on them, to take up their cross, and let their light shine before men, instead of hiding it under a bushel. She saith that one of the greatest hindrances to women's growth in grace in Bath is their reluctance to wear sober apparel in the midst of so much glistering raiment, not of angels. And I can well believe it true. It grieves me to see how my poor Patty is now bedizened; but when I spake to Mistress Spaull about the matter, she answered that the clothes came out of her pocket, and that she must dress the child to please the eyes of her customers, and not as if she was Noah's granddaughter just landed from the ark. This flippancy the poor woman mistakes for wit, and doubtless 'tis in accordance with what passeth for such among her fine customers. Mistress Saunders heard Mr. Wesley first preach in the open air at Bristol (therein following Mr. Whitefield), and saith that at first he seemed half-ashamed of his field preaching; but that, as he warmed to his work, this went off, and he soon proclaimed the mercy of God in Christ with great fluency and boldness.

Fri. 21.—I had marvelled that the Vicar, of whose rage against the wondrous work here, in which God hath deigned to make me an humble instrument, I was well advised, had not before striven to let it, but to-day, at his instance, I was brought before two Justices, the constable using more violence than was necessary; for, indeed, there was cause for none, since I went with him quietly, as needs I must, although at great inconvenience to my worldly business. I know little of the niceties of the law, but, methinks, the two Justices knew less, and that the Vicar's lawyer, one Mr. Minchin, brought from Bath, played on their ignorance in order to bring against me a hotchpotch of accusations. First, I was told that I must forfeit a shilling for every Lord's day I had absented myself from church—"and sure," said one of the Justices, thinking to show his wit, "if you be so wondrous good a man, you'll not grudge that, for 'twill be given to the poor. 'He that hath pity on the poor lendeth unto the Lord,'" he drawled through his nose. "Bean't thic good Zcriptur, pearzon?" he added, turning to the Vicar; and, indeed, all his talk was of like illiteracy.

Next they gave me to understand that if I contumaciously persisted in absenting myself from my parish church for another month, I must pay £20 to the King, and £10 a head for my wife and children likewise absenting themselves. But here the Vicar put in his word. "Nay, nay," said he, "'twould serve the saucy stubborn fellow right to punish him with utmost rigour of the law, but if we bear too hard upon him, 'twill punish them who would come to church right willingly, an he would suffer them." To all this I answered quietly that myself and family were constant church-goers—none more so. "A lie!" shouted the parson. "Deny, an thou dare, thou wert wandering about drunk on Fast Day." "'Tis a railing accusation," I replied, "and Fast Day fell not on a Sunday." Winking at his employer, who showed much confusion, Lawyer Minchin suddenly asked me whether I called myself a Quaker, and when I had answered "Nay," then he cried, "We will swear him on the book. Thou mayest be harmless as doves, Mr. Pidgeon, in thine own conceit, but, methinks, thou hast not the serpent's wisdom, though thou mayest have its venom. Wilt take the oaths of allegiance and supremacy?" "I am willing," I answered. "What, and subscribe the declaration.

against Popery?" he thundered. "Even so," was my reply.

"Don't believe un, your worships," shouted the landlord of the *Blue Boar*, who had followed me into the justice-room, glad of heart; and none even lifted a finger to silence him. "Ay, though," he went on, grumbling, "he'd swear his head off, but you needn't believe un none the more. Who heeds what a Papish swears? He's a Papish, or else he's a Presbyterian, and they're both tarred with one brush."

Having let him have his say out without interruption, the lawyer turned sharp upon me. "Do you call yourself a preacher, Mr. What's-your-name?" he asked. I answered that, as he well knew, my name was Pidgeon, and that at times I expounded the Word of God to them that were willing to listen unto me. "Ay, and to them that beänt," cried out the Justice, who thought himself a wag. "I've heerd thee bawling, little to my liking." And at this, of course, there was a great laugh. When it had died away, the man who raised it laughing longest, the lawyer said to me, "Mr. Preacher, have you subscribed the articles of religion mentioned in the statute of Elizabeth?"

"I have subscribed no articles," I answered. He interrupted me with a mocking "Ha ha, I knew that I should have thee first or last," and an inquiry whether I were willing to subscribe to the articles.

"I am a member of the Church of England," I replied, "and, therefore, willing to subscribe to any of her articles. What are those of which you speak?"

"Those," saith he, "which concern the confession of the true Christian faith, and the doctrine of the sacraments as taught by the Church of England."

"With all my heart," said I, "will I subscribe to these."

At this, changing his tone to one still more sneering, he rejoined, "Come, now, tell the truth, for once in thy life, Nathaniel. Art not an Anabaptist, Nathaniel?"

"What is an Anabaptist?" I inquired.

"Sure, Mr. Preacher, you're a bungler at your trade," he answered. "If I've to teach you divinity, you must pay me my fee. Though Anabaptist doctrine is devilry, not divinity. Why, a fellow who wants to damn babies by putting off their christening, and to make grown folk catch their death of cold by dipping them who have been sprinkled, as is reasonable, in their youth."

"I am a Pædobaptist," I answered. Whereupon, without giving me time to say more, my learned host of the *Blue Boar* shouted in triumph, "Hear un, your washups! The la'yer's got it out of un. I could ha' zworn he wer a Baptist, or zum zuch devilry."

Taking no heed of the foolish man's interruption, I went on, "As to the mode in which the rite is to be performed, the Prayer Book saith that if the child may well endure it, the priest shall dip it in the water discreetly and warily."

Thereupon the lawyer asked me of my meeting-house. "I have none," said I, "but preach now in the open air, and anon from house to house as doors be opened."

"Doors be opened!" he exclaimed, taking the word out of my mouth to mock me; "then more licences will be wanted; and which one of them hast thou registered in the bishop's court or the archdeacon's, or at quarter sessions?"

"None," I answered, "I knew not it was necessary."

"I thought as much," cried he, "and I shall bring proof, your worships, that albeit he had obtained a licence for his meeting-house, or meeting-houses, still would he not be exempt from the statute penalties, inasmuch as he hath not preached with unlocked, unbarred, and unbolted doors; but on the other hand, hath preached with locked, barred, and bolted doors." At this iteration the Justices very wisely shook their heads, as if 'twere some great point of law indeed.

Then he called a lewd fellow, on whom we have more than once been compelled to close our doors to avoid his disturbance, who declared on oath that, having at sundry times endeavoured to enter our meetings, he had been shut out—nay, more, giving lying and self-contradictory circumstance, that I had three times assaulted him (whereas 'twas he who once laid violent hands on me), so that he went in fear of his life because of me. Thereupon I was bound over in two sureties and my personal recognisance to keep the peace towards him and all his Majesty's subjects for six months. Doubtless 'twas thought I should find none willing to become bound for me, and that thus I might be committed to spend my Christmas holidays in prison; but Mr. Saunders, who had ridden over from Bath to inquire what had happened to me, became one. The other, to the vexation of the Vicar, and the astonishment of the lawyer and his brother magistrates, was, of his own offer, the Justice who kept the mob off us at Robert Farrant's. He loves not Methodists; but he is an upright man who abhorreth unrighteous judgments. I must write to Mr. Wesley touching this matter of licensing and the rest. He knows the law, and fears not to put to shame them who, from ignorance or malice, would wrest it to the injury of the innocent.

Mon. 24.—The Vicar hath made another essay to lock me up. Mr. Saunders having shut his shop until after Christmas, in order that I might redeem the time because the days are evil, I walked to a neighbouring village wherein I had heard that a few were anxiously inquiring the way to Zion. Scarce had I gathered them about me in Widow Leigh's cottage, when in walked one who, I was told, was an Overseer of the Poor, with two constables.

"Is your name Pidgeon?" asked the Overseer.

I answered "Yea."

"Bring him along. 'Tis the rogue we want, then!" cried the Overseer to his men.

As they approached to lay hands on me, I demanded sight of their warrant.

"We'll warrant ee," said the bigger constable, smiting me with his staff; but the Overseer, pulling a paper from his pocket, read his authority to bring before Mr. D—— the Rector, a great friend of our Vicar's, hunting and drinking, dicing and card-playing with him, one, Nathaniel Pidgeon, described as an able-bodied vagrom of no lawful calling going about the country to the breach of the King's peace.

"We've been looking for thee," said the Overseer, "and now thou'st walked into the gin. Bring the lazy rascal along. His zhoulders are full broad enough to carry a knapzack. There's no Methodees here to rescue un, and he zhan't come here to make none, says pearzon."

Accordingly I was haled before the Rector, the Justice who had issued the warrant, sitting alone. When I had answered to my name, giving me no opportunity to make reply or call witnesses, he abused me until he was out of breath, using oaths which would have cost him many a crown, methinks, if, like an upright judge, he had convicted himself of profaneness upon his own hearing, or the constables had done their duty, and carried him before another magistrate. 'Twas horrible to think that such language should proceed from lips commissioned to read the pure words of Scripture, to offer pious prayer to God, and preach the holy Gospel. "Out of the same mouth proceedeth blessing and cursing. My brethren, these things ought not so to be. Doth a fountain send forth at the same place sweet water and bitter? Can the fig-tree, my brethren, bear olive berries? either a vine figs? So can no fountain both yield salt water and fresh." I marvel what would his Reverence make of that passage, an he took it for his text. My judge was my accuser. He called me idle fellow, and said that those who could not labour were not fit to live. He would put me in the way of pretending to earn my bread, he added, but expressed a charitable hope that the King might not be troubled long with so bad a bargain. 'Twas not enough to call me idle, I was disorderly as well, a rogue and vagabond—yea, an incorrigible rogue, to boot. Whipping and imprisonment were too good for me; I should be transported. He would commit me, he said, and was in two minds as to whether he would not fine Widow Leigh forty shillings for harbouring of me. I was a rebel in my heart, and willy nilly should be made to serve the King. If the Pretender came, said the fair, reasonable, reverend Justice, I would be shot one way or other, most like for deserting, and 'twould be a good riddance of bad rubbish.

In vain I pointed out that I had a fixed habitation, and was well known in this village.

"Ay, better known than trusted," quoth he.

"But, sir——" said I.

"Say 'your Washup,' fellow!" cried the big constable, shaking me.

"But, your Worship," I went on, "'tis notorious that I am employed in a post of trust by Mr. Saunders, whom, doubtless, you know; him who hath his shop in Southgate Street in Bath, a man of substance and repute, my surety on another charge. Let me but send for him."

"Nay," saith the Rector, "my people have something better to do than run thy errands."

In vain was all my protestation.

"'Tis cheap to talk," cries his Reverence. "Lying comes easy to thee, Pidgeon. 'Tis thy trade. However, thou may'st prove what thou sayest at thy leisure, an thou canst. To jail I'll send thee."

And he was about to make out my mittimus when, as luck would have it as the world says, in the good providence of God say I, in came my other surety,

Justice Wills, who had come to speak with Mr. D—— on county business. 'Twas not long after this before I obtained release, Mr. Wills in good humour warning me, as I took my departure, to mend my ways, and keep out of trouble, or he would no more be bound for me; and Mr. D——, half in jest and half in earnest, growling that he had scared the vermin off his manor for one while, and, if I came again, he would take care I should find no friend at court. And such men are called Justices! When, on my return home, I related what had happened to my family, my little Jack appeared half vexed that his father should have been unwilling to go for a soldier if the King wanted him, but, thereupon, his mother, who mostly takes great pride in Jacky's high spirit, as she calleth it, chid the little lad with, methinks, overmuch heat, saying that 'twas pity that papa, who might hold his head as high as any an he would, laid himself open to be pressed for a common soldier. The pride of life hath sad grasp upon my poor dear wife. Perchance, if I would do as many men do, who, nevertheless, are held of good repute, I might advance myself in this world; but, sure, 'tis better to think of the next, and be little and unknown below for conscience sake. Jacky, unaccustomed to his mother's rebuke, began to pout, whereupon the little Susan, who had looked upon him strangely when he showed his wish that I should go the wars, ran to kiss him, and then ran back to me as if to show she did not side against me, and then to her mother for an embrace, and so continued to run backwards and forwards for a time, as her pretty, simple manner is, fearing that one or other might be jealous of her affection. She hath a loving heart. Later in the evening, to our joy, Patty came in to spend her Christmas with us. She is taller but thinner than when she left us. She makes no complaint, however, of scant food, or hard work. On the other hand, I fear the poor child loves her place but too well for the sake of its vanities. One would believe the simple wench thought herself a fine lady from the way she talks and minces. 'Twas a hardship, forsooth, to her ladyship that she could find no better conveyance for herself and box than the carrier's cart. May she never find a worse. In the presence of her mother, moreover, she takes it upon her to correct the children's manners, and my wife, although not well liking it, saith nothing, thinking that Patty hath picked up the latest fashions in behaviour.

But 'tis no theme for jesting. I am sorely grieved at her extravagant and ridiculous mode of dress, to my thinking, whatever Mistress Spaull may say, quite out of keeping with her station; and to note her love of it, and the envy the sight of it hath raised in Hester's heart. I had to reprove the poor children for their idle talk which

I overheard touching beaux and billets, and such like folly. Thank God the world hath not yet rooted out from Patty's heart all love of her home, and I trust 'twill be so with Hester likewise when she hath to leave us. When awhile since the Christmas bells rang out, 'twas comforting to have all who are closely near and dear unto me under one roof again. God grant that we may meet again next year, and, above all, that we may be a united family in heaven.

Tues. 25.—We have had a quiet day, to the small content, alas! of my elder children, who would fain have been merrier, as they name it. If the kingdom of heaven is like unto leaven which leavened the whole three measures of meal, verily, so likewise is the kingdom of the Devil. My poor Patty's pert speeches have in so short a time told upon my whole family.

"Sure, papa," she says, "there can be no sin in doing as other folk do, so long as we break none of the commandments." Poor, foolish child! Is not the man of purest life, judged after the law, yet guilty of all? And who, indeed, can say that there is but one point in which he hath offended? Verily, I have sinned in suffering the child to be bred as a milliner. Dreading my wrath she speaks not openly, but great is my fear that in her heart she holds with the fashionable folk who frequent her mistress's shop, and who, 'tis said, have well-nigh given up scoffing at the faith of our blessed Lord and Saviour Jesus Christ, as being a silly dream so often flouted that the jest is stale. I overheard my poor child mocking at the joys of heaven. "Hester," quoth she, "wouldst wish to go to heaven, to sing psalms and say thy prayers all day and night for ever and ever, Amen? 'Tis well enough to go once a week to the Abbey, to look at the fine ladies and the beaux—ay, and to be looked at, too, Mistress Hester; some of their great beauties envy me my face, and Mistress Spaull saith that I have a genteeler figure than the best of them—but a single week of psalms and sermon even there would sicken me."

Her flippant, frivolous, profane talk cut me to the heart. I must speak with her mother as to the cancelling of her indentures, at whatever detriment to her worldly interest. "What shall it profit a man if he gain the whole world, and lose his own soul?"

Thurs. 27.—This day mine own holiday ended, but wishing to gain time for counsel as to what were best to be done for our Patty, I went before business to the Churchyard to crave leave for the dear child to remain with us until the beginning of the approaching week. Mistress Spaull readily granted permission, and was in very gracious mood, wishing me the compliments of the season, and pressing me to taste her cordial. "'Tis but cherry brandy, Mr. Pidgeon," she simpered. I fear, alas, from the look of her eyes, that it had far more of the brandy than the cherries in it. I had not thought before that she was a woman addicted to strong waters. So early, moreover, in the day. This discovery makes me still more disturbed about my child, not that I fear that Patty would ever take to drink. From that, fearing its effects upon her looks, her vanity would save her—one devil casting out the other. O God, guide thou my steps. For the sake of thine only-begotten Son, our Lord Jesus Christ, let my dear child be brought to the knowledge of the truth.

X.

Fri. Dec. 28.

THIS evening I called on Izaak Wellow, and had much talk with his sister, who hath been tarrying with him during the holidays. I was glad to be of some comfort to her, but her views of spiritual matters are very dim, for she hath not yet spiritual discernment. She is evident a decent woman, sorely tried in her home. She may well need more comfort than this world can give her, and she is groping for it all but blindly, scarce as yet even seeing men as trees walking. O Lord, lay Thou Thy hands again upon her eyes. Make her look up, and she shall be restored, and see Thine whole truth clearly. Her husband is a squatter by the Quantocks. Nominally he lives by turf-cutting and brooming, stealing his heather from the moors and his sticks from the wood which first comes handy. A strange, wild, idle race these squatters would seem to be, herding together like pigs, and as ignorant of God as any heathen. Hating regular labour and restraint, moreover, as much as any of the Red Indians of whom Mr. Wesley tells. Those who try to hire them at fixed wage for ought but turf-cutting, soon give it up as a vain effort. In half-a-day or less these English wild men, weary of their whim, fling down their tools, and go back to their hovels in the wilderness. The children cut thistles for the farmers, and work in the turf, as do the women, they and the children dividing the square slabs the men have cut, and piling the turfs up into what they call their hiles and ruckles. The children run about with scarce a rag to cover them, and paddle like ducks in the black ditches. To reach their homes they must either wade or leap, since even a plank for a bridge can scarce be found. The women and children pick whortle berries, and peel withies likewise, cut in beds belonging to poor folk like themselves. In time of flood, the flooded-out folk huddle into huts that were too full before: so 'tis little wonder that in a county which holds chastity in so slight esteem, if only marriage in time prevent the birth of a bastard, modesty amongst women is scarce known. The men help themselves to the wild fowl and the tame geese in the marshes, and sometimes they make bands to hunt the red deer on Exmoor. Wellow's sister, poor woman, described to me her loathing of the wild life into which she had brought herself by her imprudent marriage, and, although she hath now lived upon the moors for the best part of her life, she says they have never yet seemed to her a home. She rejoices that she hath never born a daughter. Her sons, she says, although headstrong young men, fearing not God, nor regarding man, treat her in their rough way with kindness, but her husband, who is scarce ever sober, cider there being plentiful and cheap, often beats her when they are away.

But what is most lamentable is that these squatters know nothing of a God in Christ. Nay, 'tis to be doubted whether they have any notion of a God. Most like they never trouble themselves to think of whence they came or whither they are going. The marsh colts about them have as much divinity as they.

Yet are they very superstitious. That witches have been, no one who believes God's Holy Word can doubt; and he who believes not that hath no right to pass an opinion on ought That some are still suffered to live, only he who hardeneth his neck and stoppeth his ears against honest men's testimony will dispute. But 'tis idle as cruel to take every ugly, mumbling old woman for a witch; and exceeding cruel and absurd is the Quantock people's remedy for witchcraft. They roast a cat alive. And again, although the King's Evil may be in an especial manner a disease that can be cured by prayer (else why did the Healing Service ever find a place in the Prayer Book?) yet 'tis manifestly ridiculous to suppose, as do these poor Quantock people, with no rubric to show for it, that the afflicted person may be made whole by putting bread and cheese in a handkerchief upon the coffin, when the words "Deliver us from evil" are read at a burial.

Sat. 29.—I had thought that, at least for a season, our opponents had ceased from opposing, and that we should be suffered to end the year in peace. But I have been roughly aroused from that fond imagining, doubtless for my good. Peradventure I was too much at ease in Zion, and 'twas needful that I should be stirred up from slumber in my nest.

Farmer Jeakes having professed his willingness to let us have his smaller barn, which is well-nigh empty, and to lend us lanterns to light it, I requested William Jones, as is my wont, to go round from house to house and state that it was my purpose to preach there at seven o'clock this evening. To my astonishment, William showed much reluctance, and made many excuses. 'Twas plain that he had something on his mind, but what he would not say, although often urged. At length he went or professed to go. In any case the barn was filled. But 'twas soon evident that many had come with no thought of worship; at their head Black Jack, who, 'tis said, is half a gipsy, the hostler at the *Blue Boar*. He soon beginning to make a noise, the blacksmith's man, who, before his conversion, was notorious as a bruiser, went up to the noisy fellow, and, taking him by the neck and breeches, quietly put him out, Jack wriggling like an eel, but not daring to strike, remembering former combats in which he had been worsted, although himself a famous boxer. For a short time there was peace, but soon powder was let off, now here, now there, the smoke filling the building, and some of the straw catching fire. 'Twas providential there was so little of it, or the barn might have been burned down. In the confusion there came a shower of missiles from another mob outside the doors, and two of the lanterns were smashed. When the air had cleared a little, and we had hung up fresh lights, I began again, but then there rode in a foolish fellow mounted on an ass with his face to the tail, and, so seated, he rode the beast at me wherever I might take my stand, protesting that he could not see his way before him. My champion was still busy with Black Jack outside, or he had not so long been suffered to do it with impunity. When the blacksmith's man came in the fellow soon righted himself, and, whanging his ass's ribs with his cudgel, galloped out, the ass getting more blows and kicks from them on whom it trampled. Poor beast, I pitied it its cruel belabouring, and likewise its dishonour, when I thought of Him who came riding upon an ass, and upon a colt, the foal of an ass. Once more I essayed to speak, but was pelted with rotten eggs, and as I remonstrated with the people on their filthily unmannerly behaviour, " Here's new milk to cleanse thee," shouted a fellow, and he emptied a pail of the same over my head.

'Twas hard to bear, but I thank God for putting a bridle on my lips.

"Sure, friend," said I, as though unruffled, "thou mightest have had more wit than to waste thy substance."

"Nay, nay," cried he, "'twas none of mine; 'twas Jeakes's."

At that the farmer made a rush at him to secure him, and we broke up with much disturbance, many of us being chased to our homes.

All my family were much concerned at my plight, but poor Patty seemed even more vexed at the manner in which it had been brought about.

"Sure, papa is crazy," I heard the silly wench whisper to her sister. "'Tis so low to be a Methodist." Alas! poor child, if we be not willing to be called the scum of the earth, small chance have we of entering the kingdom of heaven. 'Tis a hard saying. No wonder the dear child stumbleth at it. Her elders, who have tasted of the riches of grace, do so likewise. In my own experience I have felt how hard it is to brook affronts with what the world calls tameness; and yesterday, when Mr. Saunders had been most wrongfully, to my joy, accused of unfair dealing, and was naturally much incensed hereat, and I had reminded him of the cross which all who would be Christians indeed must take up and patiently endure, he answered hastily that he would bear such slanderous language from no man, nay, verily, though the lawing to right himself cost him never so much. Good Mistress Saunders shed oil upon the troubled waters. "Dear John," she said, "remember, 'Blessed are ye when men shall revile you, and shall say all manner of evil against you falsely, for my sake.'" In a sense 'twas for the Lord's sake Mr. Saunders was reviled, inasmuch as his accuser railed at him the more bitterly that he made a profession of piety. God grant that he always walk worthy of it.

Sun. 30.—Young Mr. S——, nephew of squire F——, called upon me in much perplexity. I had noticed him once or twice at our meetings, but had never spoken with him before. His uncle having adopted him, he hath been looked upon as his heir, but his succession to the estate depends entirely on the squire's will, and now he is threatened with disinheritance.

He tells me that while eating his terms at the Temple, as they strangely name study for the bar, he and a brother Templar went for sport sake to a meeting of the

Society in Fetter Lane, now some five years agone or more. There he first heard Mr. Wesley, and was much impressed by his manner and its effect on the congregation. 'Twas a season of rebuke and humiliation before God, many falling to the ground, and finally all bursting forth in a song of thanksgiving. Finding that Mr. Wesley was to preach next morning before breakfast in Moorfields, Mr. S—— rose betimes (an unusual thing with him in those days, he saith), and found some thousands assembled there, to whom Mr. Wesley expounded those blessed words, " Ho ! every one that thirsteth, come ye to the waters," making reference to the summer sun which, though the service began at seven, was very hot, filling the air with a stifling haze. In the afternoon Mr. S—— took a wherry and was rowed to Lambeth, whence he went in a friend's coach to Kennington Common, where at five, to a still mightier multitude, Mr. Wesley proclaimed the Gospel, taking for his text " Look unto me, and be ye saved, all ye ends of the earth." Not the texts only, but great part of the sermons likewise, word for word, Mr. S—— saith he could remember for many months afterwards. But the impression they had produced upon him wore off, and he again led the gay life which, alas, is too common among young gentlemen who have not to work for their living, until about a year back. While then visiting at his uncle's, to pass the hours when heavy rain had prevented him from indulging in the sports of the field, he was led by the good providence of God to take up Thomas à Kempis's "Imitation of Christ" in the original, and to test whether he had forgotten his Latin, he began to construe the sentences. Pleased to find that he could do so with ease, he read on, when lo! as if suddenly, he saith, an unseen finger had probed a sore skinned over, but not healed, his former aching craving for peace with God, through our Lord Jesus Christ, returned. Alas, he hath not yet found that pearl of great price, although he hath sought it with many tears. Doubtless, 'tis lingering fear of man that holds him back. He still shrinks from taking up his cross and following Christ openly. He hath abstained from worldly amusements, made the Bible and books of divinity and devotion his sole study, and been instant in private prayer. He hath become a constant church-goer, and at times been present, Nicodemus-like, at the meetings of our brethren in Bath, as he hath at ours; getting, he saith, more good from our services than from aught he hears at church. At first his uncle, who hath much worldly affection for him, and at one time took much pride in him, strove to coax him out of what he calls his gloomy ways; but now he speaks roundly. Yesterday, Mr. S—— tells me, the Squire sent for him into his private chamber, and having bidden him to be seated, said,

"Nephew, the New Year draws nigh, and thou must hear my mind. If thou wilt not, at my wish, who have done so much for thee, give up thy mopish megrims, thou must leave my house. I will give thee £500 down upon the nail, and not a penny more through all my life; no, nor a penny nor an acre of my land at my death. Be well assured of that. £500 will not last for ever even in thy hands, which have become so sparing. Plenty thou couldst make spin once, and I did not grudge it; no, though to be made ducks and drakes of in a manner becoming a gentleman. If thy law will not keep thee in bread and cheese, 'tis not my fault. I paid thy fees and thy bills likewise; and heavy ones they were, both at the University and thine Inn."

Mr. S—— confesses that he doth, indeed, know but little of the law, but adds, with justice, that his uncle encouraged him in his neglect of its study, as pettifogging, save for a general smattering, which might prevent him from appearing as a nincompoop, and becoming a mere nose of wax for his low-bred clerk, when placed in the Commission of the Peace.

"At first," the Squire went on, "I winked at thy ways, because I had heard that the Methodists were secretly working for the good cause. But 'tis all moonshine 'Tis not through them the King will get his own again— the low-lived vermin. I would as soon turn my house into a rat-run as have Methodist preachers swarming in it after my death, as they would, an thou wert master, and still a Methodist. Better turn preacher thyself, and be pressed for a soldier. I'll not be thy bail. Nay, nay, I'm hale and hearty. I'll take a wife, and get a jolly little lad to laugh at his fool of a cousin who didn't know on which side his bread was buttered. Rather than let a Methodist have my land, I'd leave it to the poor. Tut, tut, there'll be no lack of better folk to leave it to. I was proud of thee, Tom,—loved thee for thine own sake, as well as my poor sister's. 'Tis well she's in her grave. 'Twould break her heart to see thee drivelling. Ay, and thy father's too. He was a man, and I had hoped his son would better him. I'll give thee till the year's out to make up thy mind. If thou'rt a Methodist on New Year's morn, out wi' ee, and no more two words about it."

I could but tell the young man that worldly wealth was dung and dross in comparison with heavenly gain; that a light earthly affliction which would be, comparatively, but for a moment, might work out for him a far more exceeding and eternal weight of glory, and urge him, if he thought it would be conducive to his growth in grace, to unite himself openly with us.

I pray that the necessity under which he is laid of making a decision may lead to the salvation of his soul;

but I have my doubts, to my great sorrow, for he is a young gentleman of exceeding winning manners. My heart was drawn out towards him. How hardly shall they who have great possessions, or the expectation of them, enter into the kingdom of heaven!

Mon. 31.—The Devil is afeared, and fights hard for his throne here, which, thanks be unto the Lord, we have shaken. It would seem as though he dreaded that, if he could not subvert our work before the year was out, he might never accomplish his purpose. I have again been in the hands of the sons of Belial, subjected to more degrading indignity and placed in greater peril of my life than on any previous occasion; but, glory for ever to His name, I have been preserved, and my soul hath continued unruffled. The Vicar shows not in these disturbances, but 'tis idle to say he is not answerable for them. I fear he actively, although secretly, promotes them, and in any case the lifting of his finger would stop them, an the mob thought he were in earnest, for though they may hold his office in slight esteem, thanks to the way in which he hath performed its functions, they look up to him as a gentleman of family and fortune, and friend of most of them which be of authority hereabouts.

Since Christmas there hath been much drunkenness in the parish; some of those who did once run well having, alas! fallen away. When faithfully, yet tenderly, I reproved poor James Mynn for the vile language he had uttered, with lips which I had heard earnestly pleading for mercy, and afterwards uttering praise, which, methought, could never wax less fervent, for the assurance of salvation which he had then obtained, he raised his arm and would have struck me had not one held his hand.

This morning I was to have preached by candlelight in Mr. Jeakes's barn. The early hour and the coldness of the weather kept some of our friends at home; but the devil had roused a busy mob of mischief-makers from their beds.

Scarce had I opened my mouth, when the sweep came up and strove to embrace me, and when I avoided him he beat me over the head and shoulders and about the legs with his bag, which, although empty, sent forth abundance of choking soot. Next, Thomas Burrows, the constable, laid hold of me and told me I must come with him.

"Whither?" I asked.

"To the *Blue Boar*," said he, "until the nearest Justice be awake."

So saying, he haled me out, roughly enough, but the mob thinking he did his office too gently took me from his hands, and dragged me along the frosty ground, so that my clothes were cut through to the skin. Coming to a horse-pond, they brake the ice with pitchforks and threw me into it on the farther side, pushing and prodding me back with their forks, nay, holding me down, head under water, when I had broken through the ice and staggered to the brink, until at length Burrows came up and pulled me out.

Then they cried I was not fit to go before the Justice, and brought the wheelwright with his cart-grease and his paint-pots to smear my wet rags with the stinking stuff, and daub them blue and red. After that they suffered the constable to take me to the *Blue Boar*, where the landlord, pretending to commiserate me, sent to my house for a change of linen and apparel, set food before me, and ordered hot drink to be prepared.

When I had shifted myself, and eaten and drunken, I felt much refreshed, and demanded to know why I was so treated, what evil I had done.

"Popery, flat Popery!" shouted the constable. "Whatever zum o' the gentry be, we be King Monmouth'z men, and wunt have no Popery, Popery, Popery!"

'Twas strange to hear him rolling that which he professed to loathe, like a sweet morsel under his rough tongue.

Soon afterwards he took his departure to see, as he stated, whether the Justice were stirring. Instantly in rushed the mob and seized me; the landlord making no resistance. Nay, with a sneer said he, "'Twas pity that you changed your clothes."

I heard the screams of my wife and children, as I was hurried past our home to the river, and my little Jacky's voice crying, "Dada, Dada;" and caught sight of the brave little lad running out of the garden gate. Black Jack knocked him backwards with a brutal blow, and straightway was floored himself by the blacksmith's man, who had not been at the meeting, but now came running up in hot haste.

I remember little more until men swung me by the arms and legs, and with a "One, two, three, and away," hurled me into the river.

The stream is swollen by flood, and must have borne me down some way before I came to the surface, where I clutched a half-drowned pollard. The blacksmith's man came off to me in a punt, and after much difficulty in poling, availing himself of a swell in the current, brought me to land, and assisted me to my house. May the Lord reward the good, fearless man! He taxeth himself with not having been at the service; but flesh is weak, none can be always vigilant; and he hath stood me in better stead, and brought greater credit to our cause than he could have done by fighting for me on land. The Lord, methinks, will forgive him for the punishment which, he tells me, without shame, he inflicted on Black Jack. The cowardly, hulking rascal, to strike my harmless boy! He hath a sad bruised head. The doctor hath put on leeches; but the poor little lad is very proud of his black eyes.

Strange to say—though, why should I say strange, when 'tis the doing of our gracious Lord?—save for a few aches and scratches, I feel but little the worse for my rough handling. I have been some hours in bed, and when I have taken further repose, I hope yet to be able to join our brethren in Bath at the Watch-night. Mr. Saunders, I feel assured, will not chide me for my absence from business when he hears what hath happened. This solemn service, which I have not yet been privileged to attend, was, he tells me, first held in London on the Friday night nearest the full moon, before or after, so that the worshippers dwelling at a distance might have her light to guide them to their homes, and to betray the lurking footpads. It began at half an hour past eight and was continued until after midnight; a deep awe, as 'tis easy to suppose, hushing the congregation at the midnight hour until, stirred by the perfect love which casteth out fear, they burst forth with their triumphant song—

> "Hearken to the solemn voice,
> The awful midnight cry!
> Waiting souls, rejoice, rejoice,
> And feel the Bridegroom nigh."

When I was brought to land, the mob had fled, thinking that they had done my business, and fearing that they had gone too far.

Her mother hath taken Patty back. The dear child showed much feeling when she parted from me. I have been over-persuaded to suffer her to return, but have still grave doubts as to whether I have acted right in so doing. I must keep my eye on the dear lass. O Thou, who never slumberest nor sleepest, make her the object of Thy watchful care!

XL.

1745—Feb. 5.

WHEN I made my last entry on the last day of the old year, looking forward to be present at the Watch-night, methinks I was vain-glorious in the satisfaction I felt at having escaped unscathed from the malice of mine enemies. The Lord hath humbled me, hath showed me that my strength is not as the strength of stones, nor my flesh brass, but that He alone upheld me in my heavy trial. That very evening I was seized with the illness which hath brought me very low. I am as weak as water. During my illness I was visited by Mr. Wesley on his way to Bristol, but I was not conscious of his presence. Doubtless, I may attribute my recovery to his earnest prayers. Praise be to God, his visit hath made a most blessed impression on my dear wife. Her rancour against the Methodists is gone, and her disrespect for them, since she hath seen and spoken with him. God grant that she may soon become one of us.

Ash Wednesday, 27.—To-day, for the first time since I took to my bed, I have attended church. As I walked thither, leaning on the arm of my wife, I passed some of my persecutors, and methought they looked upon me with eyes of shame and pity. Peradventure I ought to prosecute them for their outrageous assault, but my heart inclines to pass it over, that so I may win them to a knowledge of the truth. I will write to Mr. Wesley on this matter. Doubtless, 'twould have been my duty to prosecute the fellow who struck my boy, had he not been already so severely punished.

'Tis a solemn service, the Commination. Pure should be the lips that read it. Nay, none are pure, but he who calls down God's judgments on his fellows should be of an humble and contrite heart, most tender not to offend. How could the minister read to-day, "Cursed is he that smiteth his neighbour secretly," when 'twas he, I have been credibly informed, who set the mob on me last year? For him to gabble as he did of snares, fire and brimstone, storm and tempest to be rained upon sinners seemed blasphemous presumption. And, sure, these beautiful words should not be rattled over as they administer the oath in court: "Let us not abuse the goodness of God, who calleth us mercifully to amendment, and of His endless pity promiseth us forgiveness of that which is past, if with a perfect and true heart we return unto Him. For, though our sins be red as scarlet, they shall be made white as snow, and though they be like purple, yet they shall be made white as wool. Wherefore will ye die, O ye house of Israel, seeing that I have no pleasure in the death of him that dieth? saith the Lord God. Although we have sinned, yet have we an Advocate with the Father, Jesus Christ the righteous, and He is the propitiation for our sins. For He was wounded for our offences, and smitten for our wickedness. Let us therefore return unto Him, who is the merciful receiver of all true penitent sinners; assuring ourselves that He is ready to receive us, and most willing to pardon us, if we come unto Him with faithful repentance; if we submit ourselves unto Him, and from henceforth walk in his ways; if we will take his easy yoke and light burden upon us, to follow Him in lowliness, patience, and charity, and be ordered by the governance of His Holy Spirit, seeking always His glory, and serving Him duly in our vocation with thanksgiving."

Mon. March 11.—I have judged Mr. Saunders uncharitably. I had expected, when I returned to my work this morning to have been reminded by him of his goodness in keeping the place open for me. But not a word. He gave me a hearty welcome back to my desk, only commenting a little on the inconvenience to which he had been put by my absence, and of the expense of the temporary accountant he had hired to fill my place, naming the amount.

"But, sir," said I, "the young man's wage is less than mine would have been, so that in money you are the gainer."

"Nay, nay," he answered, "I'm not so hard as men would make me out. Dost think I'd stop thy pay because thou hast been disabled in the work of God? There is thy money up to Lady-day, with a little over to help pay the doctor's bill." And he handed me my quarter's wage, with what, for him, is a most handsome addition. I doubt not that good Mistress Saunders is at the bottom of this kindness; still 'tis very good of him, loving money as he doth, to yield to her prompting. That passage, "The Lord loveth a cheerful giver," hath sometimes led me to doubt whether, if there could be merit in any of our works, 'twould not, other things being equal, be a greater virtue for a miser to give at last, than for one of a liberal nature to give at first, the latter case involving the less self-sacrifice.

Tues. April 2.—Mr. Wesley hath writ me the following answer to my letter:

"DEAR BROTHER,—Your letter has found me at Newcastle-on-Tyne, where I have for a time been tarrying, visiting the sick, and the societies round about. I rejoice greatly to hear of your recovery, and of the work of grace which has been begun in the heart of your estimable wife. May God perfect it, and in His own good time, bring all your family to the knowledge of the truth!

"As to the matter of the prosecution of the rioters, put it before the Lord in prayer, and be guided by His light. It is hard to lay down a general rule. Awhile since, a man in this town, who had previously often abused our family, having assaulted me, I bade him come to me, confess his fault and promise amendment; threatening that otherwise I should bring him before the magistrates. He came, and is now gentle as any sucking dove.

"I have lately drawn up an appeal to the Clergy, praying them to give no heed to the idle tales of our Popery, heresy, schism, sedition, and I know not what, and to cease to stir up the mob against us as if we were mad dogs; pointing out that to call upon us to desist from preaching in private houses and the open air is the same as to bid us hold our tongues; and begging them in a word to prevent riot and give us fair trial before they condemn us, much less execute on us a sentence of club law.

"Yours in the fellowship of the Gospel,

"JOHN WESLEY."

Thurs. 4.—I have been busy in my garden, painting the pales and summerhouse, sweeping away the dead leaves, delving, raking, sowing, in expectation of my crop of pot-herbs and flowers. The wild flowers are out abundantly in the woods and green parks. Yesterday I walked therein with my Susan and Jack, and they laded themselves, and me likewise, a willing pack-horse, with sloe-blossom and daffodillies, wind-flowers and crow-foot, and I know not what. The house is still like a bower with the branches and the blossoms, although the flowers begin to fade. Would that my poor Patty, who hath been more than ordinary in my thoughts and in my prayers, would take to heart that faithful scripture: "All flesh is grass, and all the goodliness thereof is as the flower of the field. The grass withereth, the flower fadeth, but the Word of our God shall stand for ever."

Fri. 5.—This evening I visited Mistress Spaull to speak with Patty, but was told that she was out upon an errand. It was borne in upon me not to return by the churchyard, but to loiter for awhile in Orange Grove. There I soon saw my poor child tripping back with a band-box in her hand. Her dress was so exceeding gay that it seemed ridiculous. Had not her face been toward me, I had not known her, but marvelled to see so fine a lady bearing burdens and walking unaccompanied by beaux or followed by a footman. My first prompting was to call a chair. When she came to the obelisk she stopped and looked around, when up came a grand gentleman in a red coat, daubed with gold lace. Thinking that he was about to offer rudeness, I hastened towards them, but found my gentleman with his hat upon his heart, bowing and making speeches like a Frenchman, to which my foolish daughter listened secretly well-pleased, but affecting a mincing indifference to them and disdain for him. From her manner it was plain she had oft heard such talk from him before, and I fear others.

"Sir, or my lord," I said, "do not demean yourself by trying to befool a simple wench. Put on your hat, and behave like a man of sense and honour. I respect my worldly superiors, and would show them all due honour, but if I find you tampering with my child, by heaven!——" I was interrupted in the threat which I was about to utter, and repent in the dust that I should have backed it with an oath. Hath not our Lord said, "Swear not at all; neither by heaven, for it is God's throne"? But I was deeply moved.

"What!" exclaimed my fine gentleman, in feigned surprise, "are you the too fortunate parent of that paragon of her sex, that peerless young gentlewoman?"

"Your peerless paragon," said I, "is a simple man's

daughter, 'prenticed to a milliner, and, therefore, no fit company for lords. I hope to see her wife to an honest man.—Come with me, child," I added, taking her by the arm, and leading her away; "and never again listen to that villain."

"Nay, do not fear, lovely Patty," quoth he, with insolent familiarity. "I will bear much from thy father, because he is thy father (though I should ne'er have thought it), and because of his age I will not harm him."

Harm me! My age, forsooth! The old Adam strove hard to rise. Had it not been for the graciously restraining hand of God, I should have made the whippersnapper bear more than a little from me. 'Twould have been easy to send his threadpaper lordship skipping. O God, again I thank Thee for Thy restraining grace! I led poor pouting Patty to her mistress, and related with much indignation what had happened; but she made light of it. And when I spake hotly of taking my child home at once, Mistress Spaull denied my right to rob her of her apprentice and to force my daughter's inclinations. "Dost wish to leave me, child?" she asked, turning to Patty; and Patty angrily answered "Nay." Then said her mistress, "Go, go, Mr. Pidgeon, and meddle no more in women's matters. Leave me and her mother to look after Patty."

I had thought that my wife would have been as angry

as myself, but, to my grief, the poor foolish woman talks as if in such a case matrimony were possible, and blames me for not having enquired as to the name and fortune of the gentleman. She says that though her father was only a poor curate all his life, her mother came of gentle blood, and sees not why her children should not wed it. 'Twould not be wonderful to her, she says, although it might so seem to me, who have no ancestors. Sure, I must have as many ancestors as she, and those I wot of are, at the lowest, every whit as reputable; and do we not at last all spring from Adam? The only comfort I can get from my wife's talk is her assurance that Patty hath too much self-respect to suffer herself to be fooled as some girls are. But to what practised snares may not the poor ignorant child be exposed? And is not the heart, even of the purest, deceitful above all things, and desperately wicked? O God, in Thee only is my trust.

Mon. 15.—Old Goody Blake came to see me on behalf of her son, who after being a soldier, and then working at a trade in Bristol, hath returned home suffering from the malady which caused his discharge from the army. Goody Blake and her husband are sad tipplers. The old man is well-nigh crippled in his joints, owing, it is said, to the lead which he hath drunk in with the cider from the casks, but since her son (Samuel is his name) had become, said the old woman, a bound Methodist, as she called it, I went, hoping for the privilege of fresh Christian fellowship.

I am disappointed. I trust I judge not harshly, but Blake appears to me a vainglorious man, whose chief delight is to talk of himself, and to believe that after having been a greater sinner (as tho' frequent and audacious breaches of the laws of God and man were somehow honour) he hath now become a greater saint than any man besides.

I liked not the flippant manner in which he spake of Mr. John Haime, of whom I have heard from Mr. Wesley, and through whom Blake was led to give up his open profaneness and profligacy. God grant that he may be brought to a saving knowledge of the truth. "Jack Haime," he called him, as who should say, "A well-meaning fellow, doubtless, but no such wonder after all."

'Twas in the same regiment with Mr. Haime Blake listed, the Queen's Dragoons; continuing in it until the regiment embarked for Flanders, and he, as not fit for a foreign campaign, received his discharge.

Blake told me, with more of scorn than conviction, one of the experiences which he had heard his old comrade relate. Before Mr. Haime joined the army, he was in the employ of a tanner, and when driving home a waggon-load of bark at noon, he was strongly tempted of the Evil One to curse God and die, and he did, indeed, fling up his staff toward the heaven with frightful words of blasphemy. Thereupon, as if it had descended from the blue sky, a black and brown swan, after fluttering over his head, alighted on the ground and gazed stedfastly on him; so that he was pricked to the heart.

"'Tis my belief that poor Jack was half drunk," said Blake. "Although a steady fellow in the main, he would break out ever and anon, as he hath told me he did before he listed. But Jack was ever a coward in his sins; would pull himself up before he could half taste them."

To one who hath personal experience of the mysteries of God's gracious dealings with man, why should it seem incredible that He would teach by a bird, whether naturally sent or appearing in a vision? With Him are not all things possible?

Tues. 16.—My opinion of Samuel Blake is confirmed. I shall go to him no more, unless God, to bring him to a knowledge of his need of a Saviour, visit him with severer affliction than that which he now suffers. Unless in that case, I can do him no good, and he doth me none. In common honesty I cannot but note his shortcomings, and to take register of one's neighbour's failings without attempt at improvement doth but engender a censorious, pharisaic spirit in the observer.

Yet, alas, can it be possible to doubt that there is no true love of holiness in one who swells, not the sinfulness, but the number and character of his sins, out of a mad desire to brag? Some of the vile deeds of which Blake boasted to me to-day, 'tis manifestly impossible, from his circumstances, he could ever have performed. Again, when speaking of his youthful precocity in vain language, piling up oath upon oath with ingenious superfluity of naughtiness, like story upon story of a Babel Tower of blasphemy against heaven, he would fain, had I not stopped him with, methinks, righteously stern rebuke, have given me a sample of his devilish skill. Marvellous is his inconsistency. Although making light of supernatural manifestations as accompanying other men's conversions, he, to show himself as a brand plucked from the burning by specially saving grace, hath (I must needs say) invented one for his own so monstrous extravagant that I cannot write it down through fear of blasphemy. O Lord, open his eyes.

XII.

Sun. April 21.

 HAVE again ventured into Mr. D——'s parish, and he hath been true to his threat that he would show himself my enemy when, as he thought, I had none to help me; but the Lord hath made the wrath of man to praise Him, and the remainder thereof doubtless He will restrain.

After preaching to a little congregation on the common, gathered about the finger-post where the four ways meet, I went to Evening Prayers. The Parson, it seems, had but just heard of my audacity, and scowled at me from the desk, as if he would fain nail me to the seat until he could come down to wreak his vengeance on me, or blight me where I sat.

Scarce giving himself time to take off his surplice, he came after me as I left church.

"So, so, you are come again, Mr. Preacher," said he,

when he had first roughly stopped me, and then made me a bow of mockery. ('Twas easy to see that he had drunk freely of other than the Sacrament wine.) "What Bishop gave you orders and licence to intrude upon my parish, and privilege to wear your fine blue suit? Whoever his lordship be, he pays you well—'tis better cloth than mine is of." (Sure, 'tis not necessary to ask a Bishop's leave to wear blue clothes.) "I trust 'tis stout, for you must sit some hours in the open air, and the evening breeze blows keen. Off to the stocks with the rascal, constable."

So two constables pounced on me, and took me to the stocks, just outside the village, on the edge of the common where I had preached, hard by the cage; the Parson going with them to see it done, and a great crowd accompanying. When my feet were made fast, the Parson went away, and the crowd began to jeer.

"Nay, my friends!" I said, "if you find entertainment in seeing me sitting here for no just cause, peradventure it would please you better to hear me speaking for your benefit."

"Hear him!" cried some of those who had been noisiest before; and making of the stocks my pulpit, I declared to them the counsel of God with exceeding plainness of speech, so that deep seriousness, yea, I may say awe, fell upon my hearers.

Marvelling that none had returned to the village, Mr. D—— came back, and finding how matters had turned out, hastily bade me be released. This was done right willingly, but then the crowd would have had me tarry still to speak to them. Thinking, however, that good seed had already been sown, and not wishing needlessly to bring any into disfavour with one able and willing to injure them in their temporal affairs, I bade them a hearty farewell, which they, in spite of the presence of their Parson, as heartily returned. To Thy Name, O God, be all the glory. O Lord, water Thou the seed which Thou hast sown by the mouth of the meanest of Thy servants.

Sat. 27.—'Tis strange that here, where once there was such deadness to all spiritual things, there should have arisen a strife of tongues as to the mode of our salvation. 'Tis better than the previous stagnancy; nevertheless, 'tis a great hindrance to the progress of our work, although Samuel Blake, who hath now recovered sufficiently to leave the house, takes great delight in wrangling. I trust he will soon return to his trade in Bristol. Methinks 'tis not the part of a Christian man, if able to work, to burden his aged parents with his maintenance. For myself I care not for religious controversy. I will know nothing of Calvinism, or Arminianism, or Moravianism, but will preach Jesus Christ as I find Him in the Bible, and to mine own soul,—the Saviour of the world, crucified for all mankind, able to save to the uttermost. 'Tis we who reject God's bounty, not He who limits it. Strange that the Calvinists will stint and straiten what He hath made so free and wide, for doubtless there are among them good and faithful servants of the God and Father of us all. As for Samuel Blake, I fear he hath accepted the pestilential Antinomian views, or is fast tending thitherward. So possessed is he with a spirit of pride, so self-assured, so loose in his morality, so given to rail at them which have accepted a simple Gospel in simplicity, to hold up to scorn them which have been nursing fathers and nursing mothers to these babes in Christ. Oh, if such be the fruits of controversy on matters of religion, long may it be far from me!

Sun. 28.—This night, when I looked forth upon the stars shining in their calm or glittering brightness, methought how much more to the purpose is what the Bible tells us of them than that which I have read is the opinion of the modern astronomers. I had long secretly been suspicious of their calculations, but had not ventured to speak out; supposing the matter to be beyond my mathematics, who am but a plain, although accurate, arithmetician. Therefore it gave me great satisfaction to be confirmed in my doubts by the authority of Mr.

John Wesley, on the occasion of my ride with him from Glo'ster.

"Friend," said he, "I verily believe they know but little more of the matter than yourself or any other plain man who hath eyes in his head. Blind leaders of the blind are these wise star-gazers, who would be thought to see so much farther into space than their neighbours."

And then Mr. Wesley told me that some of them affirm the sun to be ninety, others only three, millions of miles distant from the earth. Sure, this can scarce be called an exact science! Suffice it for me to read, "When I consider the heavens, the work of Thy fingers, the moon and the stars which Thou hast ordained, what is man that Thou art mindful of him? and the son of man that thou visitest him?"

Fri. May 10.—Methinks that Samuel Blake loves an idle life. For his hands, that is to say; he giveth his tongue but little rest. After his return to Bristol, he hath come back again, as one yet too weak to labour, but bringing with him a new doctrine, which he busies himself in proclaiming with great confidence; he is now ever dinning in our ears that we should be still. I begin to pity, rather than blame, the poor man, as deficient in his intellects; so is he carried about with every wind of doctrine. 'Tis a devil's doctrine, like his other, he hath got hold of now, in spite of its seeming quietness. As far as I comprehend their mystic jargon, these Still Brethren teach that we should use no means of grace, neither read the Scriptures, nor go to church, nor fast, nor take the Sacrament, nor pray in secret, nor do good to men's bodies, nor strive to do good to their immortal souls, but do nothing but sit still with our hands folded in our laps, quietly waiting for Christ (save that we may with great clamour command others to sit still, if they begin to bestir themselves). Sure, Satan must have cut out this lazy-bed religion of set purpose to fit poor Samuel.

Sat. 11.—Alas, alas! when in this house shall we ever know peace again? All day long have I been hurrying to and fro, but to no purpose; and could I have got upon their track, 'twould not have availed to save my child from shame. Yet shall not the misguided girl be suffered to continue to lead a life of sin. None shall have rest until I get wind of them, that I may pursue them, snatch my ill-fated daughter from the arms of the villain who hath betrayed her, open her eyes to his villany, and make him cower before my avenging wrath. Alas, alas! might she not refuse to believe me? choose to continue in her fool's paradise until she shall be cast out of it, as full soon she will, by his own act? Alas, how can I sufficiently punish him? How can I punish him at all, being the great man he is, save with mine own hand? O God, do Thou avenge my cause; and deliver me from blood-guiltiness, O Lord. Tho' I oft reproved her, my Patty was dear to me as the apple of mine eye, and, in spite of her frivolity, oft showed me great affection. It cuts me to the heart that when we last parted 'twas in anger. Would that then I had carried by force my lost lamb to the fold! Her mother and I are punished for the pride we took in her good looks. Would that she had been seamed with small-pox ere she came to such a fate! It angers me that my wife, foolish woman! still talks half-complacently as if marriage might be possible. This morning Hester received the following billet, which shows, alas! that my eldest daughter likewise knew of things of which I knew not, and the mischief their mother's foolish talk about their gentle blood hath bred:—

"Dear Hetty,—Ere you receive this, I shall be hastening to my union with the most generous of men. I say not that I regard Lord —— with the feelings I might at last have been brought to bestow upon Fidelio, but he will give me a grand position. Poor Fidelio must console himself. I may make use of our interest in his favour. Be sure that I will not forget my own family. Poor dear papa may yet rejoice that on one side 'tis of gentle blood. Lord —— says that he would have had me though I had been a milkmaid with twenty such fathers; but I will not have a word said against poor papa. 'Tis through no fault of his he is not so well-born as his wife and children. Still 'tis a comfort to have good blood. His Lordship will be open-handed in matters of money, but he doth not derogate in marrying me. We match on equal terms. He hath blood, and lands, and gold, and I have blood and more than ordinary beauty. 'Twould be ridiculous to affect to doubt it after what I have seen of the fashionable world. Save that he hath not the genteel air, poor Fidelio hath far more good looks than my good Lord can claim; but looks matter not in him. My dear mamma will rejoice in my prosperous marriage. To her and my poor dear papa present my assurances of continued affection. My love to the girls, and a kiss for dear little Jack. My Lord saith he shall soon have a pair of colours. Our marriage must for the present be kept secret, until our noble father, the Earl of ——, who is not of so liberal a disposition as his son, be reconciled to my lack of fortune. 'Tis not a hundred miles from Bath, though, we shall be wed, and then we go—but whither, yet I must not say. 'Twill be paradise, save for the thought of the torments of poor Fidelio. God grant he do not drown himself.

"Your fond LADY MARTINA."

Martina, forsooth! Poor Patty! must thou change also thy baptismal name? I blush to have given being to one so blind. Nevertheless, even now 'tis hard to keep back a bitter smile at the child's childish ways. The worst of the matter is that vanity hath brought it all about. Such love as an honest woman should give a man 'tis plain the girl hath bestowed (altho' mixed with much vanity) on him she calleth in her mincing foreign talk her poor Fidelio. I must discover him. 'Twas sad, too, to note that 'twas envy, caused by what she fondly thought her younger sister's advancement, which prompted Hester so readily to blurt out the business of the letter. O my God, Thou hast brought me to the dust. To have daughters who immodestly put illicit gain before godliness! I would humble myself before Thee and search my heart to find what negligence on my part hath brought on me this sore affliction. My wife angers me with her smirking talk of marriage, thus leading my unfallen children into like temptation. Have I taken a fool to my bosom, and begotten offspring in her likeness? When I enquired of Mrs. Spaull she professed that she knew nought of what had become of my child. Peradventure she is not avised, inasmuch as she appeared vexed in good earnest that she should so soon have lost one whom, she frankly owned, she had hired as a lure to her shop. Oh, why did I suffer her to be placed with that vile woman? and permit my foolish wife to over-persuade me to permit her to tarry in the shop against my judgment? But 'tis cheap crying, "Oh, why was it permitted?" against another, when we ourselves are answerable. 'Tis the part of a weak fool, too cowardly to bear due share of common fault; in this case, mine by far the greatest. Patty's late mistress would have given me her coarse comfort. "I am sorry, Mr. Pidgeon," she said, "for you and for myself; but tut, tut, 'tis after all no such crying matter. Not one of my girls but would give her eyes (if then she could still please) to be in Patty's place. His Lordship's whim is like to last for a while—make hay while the sun shines; and when he wearies of her, he will leave her well provided. He is a free-handed gentleman."

Would that the vile woman had had a husband, that I might have smitten him to the earth for his wife's saying!

O Lord, whither is my wrath carrying me? Oh, bring back to me my child!

Sun. 19.—A week hath passed, but we have heard nothing of our child. 'Tis more bitter to have lost her thus, than had God taken her to Himself. But nay; dying in her present state she had certainly perished, and we been parted for ever; whereas now, God may be graciously pleased to bring her to repentance. O

Lord, may it be soon; and stir me up to double earnestness in seeking the salvation of all my family, and let me not make of my sorrow an excuse for neglecting the souls of others. To my shame be it written, I have not once preached, or attended the meetings of our little society, since my daughter's flight; partly because a weight was on my spirits, disinclining me to speak, and partly from a sense of shame. But I must take up my cross and once more labour in the vineyard.

Mon. 20.—This evening a gentleman, who lies to-night at the Blue Boar, sent for me and would have had me drink a bottle of wine with him, in order that he might, as he said, enjoy my conversation. I declined to drink, but tarried with him some time in, I trust, profitable talk. He had heard of my preaching and persecutions from the host, and wished to see and question me for himself.

"Who gave you licence to preach?" said he. "The Lord Jesus Christ," I answered. "But do you think it worth your while to subject yourself to such scurvy treatment as I hear you have endured?" he asked again. "Indeed, sir, I do," I replied. "Such treatment is a trial to the flesh, and it is not right that unruly men should be allowed to break the law with impunity. But I trust I am prepared to endure ten, yea a hundred fold what I have at present suffered, if I might but bring one soul to Christ." "'Bring a soul to Christ:' what mean you?" he asked. "To a sense of its need of salvation, and to its Saviour," I answered. "But this preaching in the open air, I cannot hold with it," the gentleman went on. "Sure, sir," I replied, "what our Master did, His servants need not be ashamed to do. Was the Sermon on the Mount preached beneath a roof?" "But," he insisted, "how can you, being a plain man, preach without book, when the clergy, who have been bred at the University, need written sermons? It must be disjointed rant you talk." "Sir," I replied, "although I am, as you say, a plain man, and can make no pretence to any familiar acquaintance with the learned tongues, yet have I received a fair education, and in what I have retained of it need not, perhaps, shrink from a comparison with some of our clergy. A man may have been to college, and yet turn out a dunce. But 'tis not to my own wit I trust when I preach, but to Him who hath promised the inspiration of His Holy Spirit." "And you pray, too, without book, they tell me," he said. "I would fain hear a prayer without book. I never heard a prayer without book." Taking him at his word, I asked him to kneel down with me and offered up earnest supplication to God on his behalf. He was much moved, shaking me heartily by the hand when we rose from our knees, and again when he had accompanied me to the door of the inn, to the amaze of the landlord and them which were idling at the bar.

Thurs. 23.—'Tis said that Molly Siderfin at the Red House is bewitched. Being an exceeding comely young woman, she hath been much run after by them who would have become her sweethearts. One of these, John Elworthy, having been rebuffed with much scorn, took ship last year in Bristol. Two nights since he appeared to her in sleep, dripping with water, and laying his death at her door, threatened her with punishment. Having wrung out brine from his sodden garments upon her, he then took his departure. In the morning, as she was relating her dream to her mother, she suddenly became ice-cold, and stiff as though she had been turned into a pillar of salt. Next she fell upon the floor writhing and jerking up and down like a wounded snake, beating her head upon the stones, tearing her hair, foaming at the mouth, and snapping with her teeth. Afterwards she sprang up, several times striking her head against the beams of the ceiling, and twisting her limbs and body in the air as though she would fain tie them in knots. Having been prevented from casting herself into the kitchen fire, she ran out by the back-way, and was with great difficulty held back from drowning herself in the duck-pond. And thus ever since she hath continued, at intervals, to be afflicted.

Fri. 24.—I have been to see poor Molly Siderfin, and have prayed with her, but at present with no visible effect. She was in one of her fits when I went in, and 'twas frightful to behold how the fashion of her countenance was altered; none verily would have taken her for the village beauty, the Rose of ——, as she hath been called. Afterwards having been raised to a seat, she stretched out her arms, and craned her neck backwards over the chair, so that I marvelled her backbone did not break, or the chair tilt; and in that unnatural position she remained for more than half an hour. Her arms were rigid as iron bars, no chafing of her hands could bring her to herself, and when one of them was pricked with a pin she did not flinch. At last, shuddering all over as a horse shakes himself in harness, she opened her eyes, recovered her senses, and was put to bed. Verily, we are fearfully as well as wonderfully made for such things to be possible. Had sin never entered into the world, they sure could not have been.

Her mother tells me that, although never afflicted in like manner before, she hath from a child at times been strange. Being sent to draw water from the well, she came back screaming that she durst not let down the bucket, for that the devil was beckoning to her from the bottom. At other times she would tell her friends not to sit on such a chair, for that such an one (naming a dead person) was already seated in it. She hath foretold the death of several, their apparitions, before death, having been seen by her; some encompassed in golden light, and some with smoke and flames. She hath heard sounds likewise which none other could hear; sometimes heavenly music, and again groans, and wailing, and the clanking of chains. Peradventure 'twould be better simply to leave her in the hands of the Lord, who may by these mysterious means be leading her to Himself.

Sat. 25.—The very hairs of your head are all numbered. Twice within twenty-four hours hath the Lord's hand been put forth miraculously to preserve me. Going into Bath this morning, the wind blowing very high, just as I reached the ruined cottage which stands above the roadside, I chanced to look at my watch, and found to my astonishment that I was late, and must hurry on if I would be in time. Accordingly I set off upon the run, and had scarce passed the cottage when the front wall fell in upon the road before the wind. I reached Bath before my time instead of after, finding by comparison with the city clocks that my watch was fast. I have never known it to gain before since it was given me by good Mistress Saunders, after I had been robbed of my old one in my flight from Farmer Farrant's.

Her gift, again, and peradventure my life, methought I was like to lose to-night. I stayed late in communion with the brethren, and 'twas dark before I set out on my return. When half-way home, two footpads pounced upon me, who, clapping pistols to my head, demanded with many oaths my money or my life. They took from me the small sum I had on me, and my watch, and then one, disappointed with the poorness of the booty in money, would have taken from me my coat, but the other, who held the watch, rebuked him, saying, "Nay, nay, let the poor man keep his coat." "Friend," said I to him, "I have done thy bidding, and now wilt thou do mine? Let us kneel, and I will pray for thee and thy fellow." The one who had taken the money at this made off, cursing the one to whom I had spoken for a fool, inasmuch as he tarried, and knelt down beside me on the turf. I had not been more than a minute engaged in prayer when he thrust back my watch upon me, swearing that he would keep nought of mine for fear that a judgment should come upon him. Then rising hastily, he took to his heels and vanished in the darkness.

XIII.

Wed. June 12.

YESTERDAY, being in Bristol, I met, to my great delight, with Mr. Wesley, who is on his way to Cornwall. He condoled with me on our family affliction; but made me severely search my heart to discover whether I bestowed not undue affection on my children, and had not been negligent in my manner of bringing them up. In this I have not wittingly offended, but had I earlier sought the Lord, peradventure ere this my children had sought Him likewise, and my poor Patty had not been led astray.

Tues. 18.—A new report hath been bruited about concerning me; to wit, that at our private meetings I pardon sins, receiving money for my absolution. Therefore I must needs be Papist. Perchance; but if I do no such thing, what then? 'Tis strange the idle tales against us which men will credit, without one jot or tittle of foundation. As any stick will do to beat a dog with, so any accusation may be used to blacken a Methodist. Now that rumours of a descent on our shores are in the air once more, the old story of our being Pretender's men is revived with double rancour. I know little of affairs of State, but 'tis said that many of the gentry in these parts are disaffected to the House of Hanover. The people of this village, nevertheless, although, methinks, they know less of these matters even than myself, are staunch friends of King George. At which I could rejoice had they not zeal without knowledge. Ignorant prejudice having fastened the name of disloyalty upon us, it may be that we shall be hardly treated in case of invasion. But the Lord will provide. 'Tis a great hindrance to our work, this feeling against us; and some of those which once walked with us have increased it by the malicious reports which they have spread. Those with whom I once took sweet counsel together, abuse me as a sensual, self-seeking man. That he is in some matters selfish, what man could undertake fully to deny? but the charge of sensuality is, I make bold to say, gross calumny. Wherein do I offend? I have adhered to my vegetable diet, and scarce ever taste ale or wine.

Thurs. 20.—This evening there came into our meeting a vain, conceited young man from Bath, a joiner's journeyman, who, because he hath dipped into books, and acquired a smattering of French and Latin,—that is, he can make use of a few words of those languages,—thinks that the wisdom of the world will die with him. He had been drinking at the *Blue Boar*, and doubtless had been egged on by the landlord to come and make sport of us. He interrupted not our service, but so soon as it was over, using many hard words, of which, 'twas plain to see, he scarce understood the meaning, and sometimes not at all, he began to put questions, which 'twas difficult to answer, inasmuch as it was next to impossible to ascertain what he would be at. Thinking he had silenced us by his logic, he was about to take his departure in triumph, saying that he would trouble us no more for the nonce, when an old woman stopped him. "Stay, young man," said she; "you profess to know many things. Tell me this. Do you know what you must do to be saved?" At this his high looks fell, and answering her never a word, he slunk away.

Fri. 21.—A company of soldiers this day passed through the village, to the delight of little Jack, who is never weary of gazing upon the red coats, and whom, to his great pride, a sergeant took upon his knee; but to the grievous disturbance of the place. Much rudeness was shown to women, and some gardens were plundered During the whole time of their stay the soldiers were drinking, not only at the *Blue Boar*, but also at the *Dog and Pheasant*, where, being under less restraint (though little it was anywhere), they brake the windows and set the taps a-running. 'Tis pity such be our defenders, bringing on their own countrymen in time of peace some of the miseries of war. Doubtless, the soldier's is an honourable calling, and there are many Christian men in the army; but such as these bring discredit on it. Hetty tells me that she detected among the wildest the young man whom her sister calls Fidelio, a young Bath tradesman of good character, to whom, Hester confesses, Patty gave great encouragement, but who hath now broken up his shop and gone for a common soldier. Poor child, poor child, thou hast brought grief and shame on others beside thyself.

Thurs. Aug. 8.—Mr. Wesley hath visited us and put our little Society in order, appointing me a Leader. Samuel Blake he sharply reproved. In the evening he preached on the Green to, I should say, pretty nigh all the people of the place. Even the Vicar came out to listen. He made no attempt at disturbance, but methinks it was unmannerly of him to turn his shoulder and walk back to the Parsonage without a word when he saw Mr. Wesley advancing to greet him. When Mr. Wesley had begun the service, then he came out again. We had a very solemn time, and the night being very warm, though dark, we continued together until long after dusk, so that at last we could only hear, not see, the leaves rustling around us. Mr. Wesley lies at my house. The room shall henceforth be called the Prophet's Chamber. It hath been a sweet season of refreshing.

Fri. 9.—This morning, after preaching at five o'clock, Mr. Wesley returned to Bristol. Having business of my master's to do there, I rode with him. On the way Mr. Wesley spake to me of leaving my present occupation, bidding me trust my family, nothing doubting, to the care of Providence, and go forth to preach the Word; but to this, for the present, I cannot see my way clear. I know that I have not the faith of that great and good man; but this counsel seems to me to lack not only worldly but common Christian prudence. I know full well what my wife will say of such a plan if ever brought about. I must lay it before the Lord in prayer. I am more and more resolved *in everything* by prayer and supplication with thanksgiving to let my requests be made known unto God. This evening as I rode home, my nag suddenly fell lame. I dismounted, and led him, praying as I went; and in ten minutes he was able to canter as well as ever.

Mon. 12.—This day I went to the marriage of John Davis and Grace Knill, both savingly converted to God, walking worthy of the vocation wherewith they have been called. It was a truly Christian wedding; no drunkenness, fiddling, dancing, idle talk, or lascivious jesting. All present were God's people, and we spent the day in prayer and thanksgiving, mutual exhortation and conversation becoming the Gospel of Christ. Ere we broke up, a few more friends having come in, I preached. Oh, had my Patty been content with such a wedding, she were now an honest woman, and I a happy man.

Tues. 13.—A strange old gentlewoman hath visited me. She is half out of her wits, but being harmless is allowed to wander about alone, for none but a stranger would harm her, and sure he would have a heart harder than the nether millstone. Crazy Kate they call her. She hath small remains of grandeur, but her great craze is that she is still hand-in-glove with all the quality. To them, as they go by on horseback or in their coaches, she will smile and smirk, bow, curtsy, kiss her hand; and most, to humour her, answer her salute. Some will halt to speak to her. I wondered, therefore, to hear on my return from business that she should have asked in the day more than once for a plain man like myself. Soon she came in, and mincing and pulling up her cracked mittens over her lean wrinkled arms, she beckoned me out of the chamber in which I sat with my family (first pleasing my little Jack by telling him that she knew he would be a brave soldier and fight for the true King), and said that she would speak with me alone. Having taken her into the little brown parlour, she bade me lock the door. When I had done so, she took out the key, and put first her eye and then her ear to the keyhole. When she had listened awhile, she put in the key again, drew up her chair to mine, and nodded. I knew not what to say, and she mumbled

> "In seventeen hundred forty-five,
> If the good king be then alive,"

with more gibberish which I could not catch.

"Hath His Royal Highness landed?" she went on impatiently.

"His Royal Highness!" I exclaimed.

"His Royal Highness the Prince of Wales," she answered. "What news brings he of his royal father, His Most Religious and Gracious Majesty King James? Sure you must know."

"Nay, Madam," I answered; "we poor Methodists are King George's men: how should I know?"

At that she looked at me, at first in wonder and in doubt, and then, as if discovering that she had been deceived, she rose, and stamped, her withered cheeks twitching with her rage, and shook her fan at me, as if she would fain brain me with it. Then drawing herself up, and holding back her skirts, she pointed to the door, and loftily bade me open it. Susan and Jack were without, having been drawn by curiosity, and Jack came forward hoping for more praise; but at him, too, she so fiercely shook her fan that Susan threw her arms about her brother to protect him. 'Tis plain the poor old gentlewoman hath jumbled in her distraught brain the report of our Popery with those going about concerning the Pretender. Perchance she hath heard something more than ordinary let fall among the gentry. 'Tis said she was of what they call the Old Religion, tho' indeed it is a grievous corruption of the Primitive, which we would fain restore. That Methodists should be called Papist and disloyal is verily a mystery of iniquity. The doctrines which distinguish the Church of Rome from the Church of England we do most cordially abhor, and King George hath no subjects more firmly attached to his royal person and illustrious house. In all things lawful, according to God's Word, which hath enjoined reverence for rulers upon Christians, we are prepared to obey His Majesty's commands to the uttermost.

Wed. 14.—How graciously doth the Lord weave the most trifling circumstance into the web of His mysterious dealings with men! But can aught be called insignificant in a world which He hath made? Nay verily. Doubtless the strange visit which I had received before I went to bed had something to do with the dream I had last night, but it hath been blessed to my soul. I dreamed that the end of the world was come, and that being summoned to appear before the King of kings, and asked whether I could stand before His face, I answered that I knew Him not. This led me in the morning to narrow searchings of heart. That fearful passage stood out in characters of flame before my eyes: "Many will say to me in that day, Lord, Lord, have we not prophesied in Thy name, and in Thy name have cast out devils, and in Thy name done many wonderful works? And then will I profess unto them, I never knew you; depart from me, ye that work iniquity."

My self-examination led me to discover that for some time past a feeling of false confidence, of satisfaction in my poor worthless works, hath been stealing over me. But now, everlasting glory to Thy name, O Lord, I can again rejoice in free salvation, feel that I am a poor sinner saved simply through my faith in Thy risen Son, by the precious sprinkling of the blood of our Lord Jesus Christ. Surely dreams are means of grace, and, tho' 'tis fond to take all as portending future occurrences or revelations of past events, the vulgar opinion, methinks, is right in so taking them in by far the greater part of marked cases. Again I thank the Lord for His dream. Doth not the Scripture say that in them He appeareth and speaketh? Methinks I have been too ready to record here, and, peradventure, to magnify mine own experiences; forgetting how many of my brethren have been like and greater sufferers. To humble me, I will record what Mr. Wesley told me of his late sojourn in Cornwall.

On his arrival in Redruth, finding that Mr. Maxwell had been seized, Mr. Wesley and his two companions set forth to the place to which the good man had been carried, but learnt upon their way that the constables, affrighted by the likely story that a mighty mob of Methodists was coming to rescue him, had carried him two miles farther. There they found him, rejoicing in the Lord. When they came out to ride to a place called Market Jew, in order to speak to the Justices, they found the door beset, but the mob parted like water before them; none venturing to throw stones until the fellows thought they were far enough off to enable them to run away, in case Mr. Wesley should ride back. (The mob here hath not shown itself so fearful.) The Magistrates, they found, had sentenced Mr. Maxwell to go for a soldier, and sent him by boat to Penzance, where he was cast into a dungeon; having first offered him to the captain of a man-of-war, who refused to take him, save as chaplain. Another man they pressed for having the impudence to tell gentlemen that he knew his sins were all forgiven. Not having the like blessed assurance, the poor gentlemen were exceeding wroth.

While Mr. Wesley was preaching at St. Ives, the Mayor had the proclamation against riots read to disperse the throng, and afterward came a gentleman with a warrant to apprehend Mr. Wesley and his companion, which, when he had drunk off his wine, he was most unwilling to carry out. Again, at another preaching, a drunken gentleman rode up and bellowed to his men to lay hold on Mr. Shepherd, and when they could not get at him, himself laid hold on Mr. Wesley, forsooth, to press him for a soldier. Mr. Wesley quietly went with him, and when he had spent his breath in cursing, asked him by what right he was forcibly carrying him away to serve his Majesty. This brought my gentleman to his senses, and he was glad to set Mr. Wesley on a horse, and see him safe back through the rabble.

Again, when Mr. Wesley was at Falmouth, a drunken mob, amongst them privateer's men, besieged the house, and broke in the doors, but Mr. Wesley, walking out without his hat, quieted those of the rabble next about him, who then swore that none should touch him, and gentlemen coming up, he was delivered out of their hands; the only harm he got being an evil wish from one that he might go to hell. The secret of all this wrath is, as one of them confessed, that the Cornish gentlemen have spread a report that Mr. Wesley hath been travelling abroad, and hath been sent by the Pretender to raise troops for him in Cornwall. This the gentlemen swear he shall not do. More than once they dispersed his congregation by the reading of the Riot Act; and on another occasion, when preaching on a high wall, he was pushed down to the peril of his neck. But he alighted on his feet, without harm; coming down, he told me, like a bird. "He shall give his angels charge concerning thee, and in their hands they shall bear thee up, lest at any time thou dash thy foot against a stone."

XIV.

Thurs. Aug. 15.

AM again greatly exercised on behalf of my dear children. Of their general behaviour I make no complaint, but not one of them hath been awakened to a sense of sin, and they all, like their mother, retain a distaste to our services. She no longer reviles the Methodists, but her heart is not inclined, as I had hoped, towards the blessed Gospel they proclaim, and her example naturally hath great influence. I can but continue to trust that, as was said of old of St. Augustine, children of so many tears cannot be lost. I cannot censure myself with undue indulgence of them, notwithstanding Mr. Wesley was disposed to think that to be my fault. Good man though he be, he, methinks, is disposed to be too stern towards children, through lack of familiarity with their nature, and his mother, from what he hath told me of her, although she had a large family, was

exceeding strict in the manner of their upbringing. When but a year old, they were threatened with the rod if they raised a cry, so that they became quiet as so many mice. Now, doubtless, an everlasting shouting without purpose, or wailing and wrangling among children, is an odious noise; but 'tis pleasant to hear the voices of them which are modest, merry, and affectionate; and it seems an unnatural thing that a house full of them which are by nature so full of liveliness, should be, as was Mrs. Wesley's, as silent as a sepulchre. Mr. Wesley, moreover, is of opinion that it is a sin to indulge in any manner of sport. Worthy man, I cannot but smile at the fondness of this belief. Were he the father of children, more especially had he had, like myself, long experience in the training of those of others, he would know that 'tis as impossible to keep a child from playing, as 'tis to stop a tree in growing. Yea, the tree may be stopped, but 'tis by killing.

Fri. 16.—This evening I gathered a congregation on the Green. While we were singing a hymn to gather more, some one (I will name no name, not being fully assured, although I have good ground for suspicion) sent a man with a bell round to proclaim in derision, " O—yez O—yez. This is to give nottis. Now's the time to zave your zowls, for a Methodee's goan to bawl." The cry gave me my text: " Behold, now is the accepted time, and now is the day of salvation. How shall we escape if we neglect so great a salvation?" God blessed the words which were spoken, and soon the bell-ringer was one of the quietest of my hearers. But Satan was permitted to disturb us. The blacksmith dares not quarrel with his man for having joined us, not only because he stands in personal fear of him, but also because he would not willingly lose his services. He is, however, more than ever set against the Methodists since his good man became one, and his son having attended our service, he came and dragged him out from the midst of the crowd by the collar. When he had got him free, he began to horsewhip him for what he called his disobedience, so savagely that a cry of "Shame!" was raised, and he had to desist. Nevertheless, I fear the poor lad was cruelly beaten when he reached his home. This interruption sadly untuned the spirit of us all; but I trust that, in spite of it, much good was done.

Sat. 17.—The blacksmith's son having been, as I expected, severely scourged, hath run away, and no one knows what is become of him. The man lays it to my charge, inasmuch as the lad said, while receiving his flogging, that, whatever his father might do, he was resolved to attend the preaching, for he wished to save his soul. Poor lad! I do not justify his running away, but if he had been turned out of doors for his coming, gladly would I have taken him in. I must seek him. O Lord, watch over him, and perfect the work Thou hast begun. To-night I sat for a time with Sarah Black. Her sufferings will soon be over. She is fast sinking. Oh, be Thou with her when she walks through the valley of the shadow of death.

Sun. 18.—Dear Sister Black hath entered into the rest that remaineth. I was with her in her last hours. She had long lain moaning, scarce opening her eyes, save when water was put to her lips. At length I thought I heard her striving to say something in the midst of the gasping for breath which had come on, and putting down my ear, made out—

> "Christ hath the foundation laid,
>   And Christ shall build me up:
> Surely, I shall soon be made
>   Partaker of my hope."

"Is it peace, sister?" I whispered, taking her hand. "Trouble not to strive to speak, but clasp my hand in answer." She made no response, but pointed with her other hand. "She would have me pray with her," cried Sister Wood (who, methinks, is too ready to show her gift), and instantly went down upon her knees. But I saw that the poor woman was in want of water, which when she had taken, she opened her eyes, and motioned to us to raise her up. This we did, and propped her with pillows, on which for a time she lay back, panting for breath. When we had given her more water, and bathed her brow, suddenly she sat up, with her eyes wide open, and putting palm to palm looked up to heaven with a sweet smile, and said, "O Lord, receive my spirit," immediately afterwards falling back upon the pillows. So she fell asleep. It was strange to note how, in the moment of death, all the sad, anxious look which sickness had given to her face, vanished like chased clouds, revealing the blue sky, and her last smile was stamped upon her lips.

Mon. 19.—This day poor Teddy Joyce, the blacksmith's son, came to me in Bath, after wandering about with no roof to cover him since he left his home; though, indeed, this in weather so fair would have been no great cross had he had enough to eat, but save for a crust or two which he had begged at cottages, he had had nothing. Good Mistress Saunders, as soon as I told her of him (having told her before of the reason of his flight), had him into the kitchen, and set him down to the abundant remains of the beans and bacon which we had had for dinner. Mistress Saunders is a bountiful provider for the table (and to her liberality in this matter her husband raises no objection), and knowing that I was to dine with them, and that my meat was vegetable, had furnished an exceeding plentiful portion of the pulse. How can men doubt the providence of God? When Teddy entered the shop and inquired for me, Mr. Saunders was speaking to me of his need of a stout lad to run errands and act as light porter. In this capacity he engaged Edward, promising him board and lodging and a tolerable wage, in case his father consented. In any case the lad was to tarry for the night in Southgate Street. Joyce blustered a bit when I spake with him, about the wrong that was done him, who had wished to bring up the boy to his own trade, through others coming between them; but he hath been brought round. I rejoice greatly. Teddy will now be under mine own eye, and in my absence good Mistress Saunders will well look after him, so that he run not into temptation; and will water the seed which hath been sown in his heart. She is a woman of a motherly disposition, and was much moved when she heard that Edward had no mother of his own, and an unregenerate father, of so fierce a nature. The Angel which redeemed me from all evil bless the lad! 'Tis plain he hath inherited his father's hot temper; but, methinks, it will not be greatly tried in his new place.

Wed. 21.—Let him who would be saved from being wise in his own eyes keep a diary, and enter therein honestly his misjudgments. Edward Joyce hath again run away. Last night it seems, after I had left, Thompson the porter (a man of evil spirit, whom I marvel Mr.

Saunders should employ) taunted the lad, the maids say, with a wish to creep up his mistress's sleeve and step into his shoes, and called him charity brat, with other opprobrious names. Goaded to fury, the unhappy lad took up a knife, and flung it at him, but luckily it missed, and stuck into the wall. Thereupon the man chastised Edward,—lightly, say the maids, thinking, maybe, to screen their fellow-servant. Howbeit, this morning he had fled. He hath not returned to his home. When I went thither to ask for him, his father, far from sorrowing at what had happened, triumphed over me. "Thou'lt ne'er make a Methodee of Ted," said he; "what's bred in the bone will come out in the flesh. He's a chip of the old block. I could wish, though, that he had stood up to the fellow as an Englishman should, and pummelled him within an inch of his life, as I would ha' done at his age." God grant that he fall not again to the care of such a father. Mistress Saunders is exceeding grieved. Her heart had been drawn out towards Edward.

Sat. 24.—As she would give me no other opportunity of opening my mind to her, I have writ the following letter (to be left at her house to-morrow) to Jane Wells :—

"DEAR SISTER,—Be not offended at this freedom. We once took sweet counsel together, and I trust that my labour in the Lord for your sake may yet prove not utterly in vain. How is it, my sister, that, having begun to run well, you have turned aside, and again become ensnared and led away by the spirit of this world? The Lord knoweth that I would not add to your cross, but if you take not it up, how can you hope to enter into the kingdom of heaven? I know that you have had trials, being unequally yoked with one who careth for none of the things which concern our peace, and living in the midst of ungodly neighbours; but your afflictions in this respect are, indeed, light in comparison with those which some have been called to endure. For myself, had I listened to the promptings of the flesh, I should have still been a self-righteous Pharisee, instead of a sinner saved by grace, and an humble preacher of that grace to others. Hath not our Lord said, 'In the world ye shall have tribulation, but in Me ye shall have peace?' Ask the strength you need, and it shall be given: seek, and you shall find; knock, and the door of mercy shall again be opened unto you. Oh, my sister, let not your godliness pass away as the flower of the grass! For the sun is no sooner risen with a burning heat, but it withereth the grass, and the flower thereof falleth, and the grace of the fashion of it perisheth.

"'Tis less than a month since you were happy in Jesus, and now you make no profession of religion, and shun our assemblies as though we were plague-stricken. As my joy was great at your earnestness, so exceeding great is my grief at your backsliding. Although you now make no open profession of religion, I hear you say that you still have it in your heart; but be assured of this, that if you are ashamed to confess Christ before men, you cannot stop until you have given up the last remains of piety. Oh, my sister, you have begun to sin like Peter; wait not until, like him, you have cursed the name of Him who bought you, before you begin, like Peter, to repent.

"Your sincere well-wisher,

"NATHANIEL PIDGEON."

XV.

Mon. Aug. 26.

MR. WESLEY hath writ to Mr. Saunders urging him to release me from his service, that I may ride abroad to preach the truth.

Mistress Saunders, who thinks that that good and wise man cannot err, advises my consent; but Mr. Saunders is strongly set against my going. His mind was much eased when he found 'twas not of my motion Mr. Wesley had stirred the matter. My wife says 'tis a scheme fit for Bedlam, and thinks 'tis but poor behaviour on the part of Mr. Wesley to go about to rob me of my employment, and cast my family upon the parish. I have again laid the matter before the Lord, but can obtain no guidance leading me to consent. Methinks, were the support of my family assured, I would gladly go forth, had I the gifts and graces needful for so great a work. I will here put down, as a composition, the thoughts which yesterday passed through my mind :—

A Sabbath Meditation.

Of the fields, at this season, some are white unto the harvest, while in others, the ripe grain falls before the sickle. Let the sight, O Lord, stir up in our hearts a desire to take some part, however lowly, as labourers in Thy harvest. Let it remind us that they that sow in tears shall reap in joy, that he that goeth forth and weepeth, bearing precious seed, shall doubtless come again with rejoicing, bringing his sheaves with him. Let it remind us also of the last great day when the Son of Man shall send forth His angels, and they shall gather out of His kingdom all things that offend, and them which do iniquity; and shall cast them into the furnace of fire, where shall be wailing and gnashing of teeth. O Lord, let us not then be numbered with the tares, but with the sheaves which Thou hast garnered.

The birds, which have been silent since the spring, renew their songs. So, Lord, let us resume Thy too long intermitted praise, and never again forget to glorify Thee, until at length, through the riches of Thy mercy, we sing Thy praise above for ever and for ever. Amen.

Sun. Sept. 1.—It hath been decided that I shall set forth for London, to accompany Mr. Wesley for a time upon his journeys, so that under his eye I may make trial of my powers as a preacher. If the Lord provide not otherwise, Mr. Wesley hath engaged to be answerable for the support of my family during the time of my absence with him, and hath sent a bank-bill for present necessaries. They will have likewise my quarter's wages, Mr. Saunders having, at the prompting of his good wife, paid me in full to Michaelmas. He says that he shall not fill up my place, but again hire for a time the young man who served for me during my sickness, having good hopes of soon seeing me back at my old place. I leave all in the hands of the Lord.

Mon. 2.—I have to-day kept holiday, or rather, I have had a day more busy than my wont, going about from place to place to make preparation for my journey on the morrow, and provision for my family during my absence. I visited John Durand at Bellott's Hospital. Although he hath been there since Lady-day, he hath derived no benefit from the waters. I read to him of the angel which went down at a certain season to trouble the waters of the pool of the five porches in the sheep-market at Jerusalem, and of the impotent man who was made whole at last through faith in Christ, and prayed that he might have like simple trust. He must, it seems, leave his present Bethesda at Michaelmas, from Lady-day to Michaelmas being the season appointed for the poor patients' sojourn; but he hath obtained promise of admission to the General Hospital. He said that he had found great difficulty in making his eighteenpence a week of maintenance money suffice for his necessities. I fear the poor brother is of a somewhat repining spirit. But we should not judge harshly of them whom the Lord hath afflicted. The spirit may be willing, though the flesh is weak.

In Stall Street I met Lewis the verger, with a posy of snap-dragons in his hand. On my asking him where he had gathered them, I learnt to my astonishment that they grow abundantly on the Abbey tower. He gave me half for my children, taking the rest home for his own. On my way home across the meadows I gathered a sheaf of purple crocuses, so that I had a brave nosegay to share between my Sue and Jack. Dear Hetty hath a more tender heart than I had allowed her. In packing my valise her tears fell fast upon my shirts. Notwithstanding the provision which hath been made for her and for her children, poor Sarah is so set against my going, that she obstinately refused to have any hand in the preparations for my journey. O Lord, watch over her and Hester, my poor lost Martha, Joan, Frances, Susan, and John during my absence, and if it be Thy will, may we all live to meet again in health and peace. And, O Lord, make clear my way before me. Reveal to me Thy will, and give me strength to do or bear it, whatever it may be. I would fain neither thrust myself into a work to which I am not called, nor refuse to yield to a manifest leading of Providence.

LONDON, *Sat.* 7.—On Monday we set out for the North. To-morrow is the rest of the holy Sabbath unto the Lord, and throughout it I hope, God willing, to enjoy sweet peace. 'Twill be something new to be ministered unto instead of to minister. To-night, having for the first time leisure, I will set down what seems to me noteworthy in my journey. At the Devizes, which town, although I had been near to it, I had never before visited, happening to let drop the reason of my journey, I was forced to hurry on, without baiting my horse, so set are the poor people there against the Methodists. After the stone houses of Bath, 'twas strange to see a town built almost entirely of timber. At Hungerford, it is said, a brass horn is kept, given to the town by John of Gaunt, which every Hock Tuesday is blown to gather the inhabitants together for the election of a constable. I saw the famous White Horse, cut out on the side of a chalk hill, in memory of one of the old battles. Newbury hath broad well-paved streets. I stopped to bait my horse and rest and refresh myself at Thatcham. At the public table of the inn, one, whom I suppose I must call a gentleman, used viler language, and that in the presence of gentlewomen moreover, than I could have thought it possible for the lowest gaol-bird. I could not but reprove him. Whereupon, being in liquor, he drew his sword, and threatened to spit me like a woodcock, but a companion with more wit struck up his blade. In his drunken awkwardness he had nigh slashed his own face. O Lord, I thank Thee for Thy watchful care. In riding through Windsor Forest, a stag, angered I know not why, ran at me, but his horn but grazed my boot, and the nag, swerving, was not harmed at all. For all the journeying mercies vouchsafed unto me, I render thanks unto Thee, O God.

I was received by Mr. Wesley with great kindness. He had found time to procure me a bed in the house of an ancient woman, dwelling in Little Moorfields, one of God's faithful people, with whom I have held communion to the refreshing of my soul.

Sun. 8.—I have enjoyed to-day an antepast of the bliss of heaven. Scarce giving ourselves time to eat and drink, we have devoted the whole day to spiritual service, and the Lord hath been very present in our midst, filling us with all joy and peace in believing. After the evening service, Mr. Wesley invited the society to remain, that in these troublous times we might commend one another to the care of God. Mr. Wesley called upon me to engage in prayer, and, thanks be unto God, I found 'twas as easy to pour out my heart to Him before a crowd in this great city as in our little meetings at ——.

Many were much moved when Mr. Wesley spake as though they might see his face no more. Yet doth he never forget the business that lies nearest to his hand. In bidding Sister Chignell farewell, he bade her take heed to have me called betimes to-morrow. I shall oft look back with gratitude to my sojourn in her house. She is a nursing mother in Israel.

SHEFFIELD, *Wed.* 11.—After Mr. Wesley had preached, he would fain have me speak likewise. His presence was a great check upon the freedom of my utterance, and methinks he begins to doubt whether he have not been mistaken in his belief as to my vocation as a preacher. I am in the Lord's hands, and am quite content to continue little and unknown. Nay, my natural yearning is to be restored to my home and family. In tale of days I have not been long severed from them, but the time seems long to me, and I would fain see their faces once more, and minister again among my neighbours. This place standeth on hills and in valleys through which water flows, but 'tis not to be compared in comeliness of aspect with the city of Bath and the river Avon. The air, moreover, is thick with smoke. During our stay at Northampton, Mr. Wesley visited the learned Dr. Doddridge at the academy he keeps there in Sheep Street, over against the *Ram Inn*, and expounded the Scriptures to his young gentlemen. I should have esteemed it a privilege to have been permitted to accompany him, but Mr. Wesley said Nay somewhat sharply, and sent me to speak in the Market Place, and afterward in what they call the Drapery. I spake with far more boldness than to-day, although many of the shoemakers, who were most numerous among my hearers, were drunk and attempted disturbance.

Mr. Wesley had purposed to turn aside to Epworth, but the news from the North becoming worse daily, nay hourly, he hath resolved to push on to look after his family in Newcastle. Last night he gave me an account of his miraculous deliverance, when a child, from being burnt to death. 'Twas not the first time, he tells me, that his father's house had been set on fire by his parishioners, exasperated by the faithfulness of his rebukes. He told me also of a ghost, or evil spirit, which for a time was suffered to disturb the inmates of the Parsonage. Strange in so pious a home. When he hath more leisure, I must ask him to suffer me to take down a particular account of the occurrences in writing.

OSMOTHERLY, *Mon.* 16.—During our stay at Leeds we were roughly handled by the rabble, for joy, said Mr. Wesley, that the Duke of Tuscany was emperor. He likened them to the Cornish folk, who pulled down the house at St. Ives for joy that Admiral Matthews had beat the Spaniards.

NEWCASTLE-ON-TYNE, *Wed* 18.—We arrived here early this morning, and found the town in a tumult, men running to and fro like ants when their hill is stirred, for news had just come in that the Pretender had taken Edinburgh. Yesterday morning at two, 'tis said, he entered. There are many Scots in this town; yet 'tis much set against the Scots, in memory of former injuries inflicted by them, who have more than once had it in their possession and done much damage to its trade. When, in the time of the civil wars, the Scots were besieging it, the Scots' prisoners were put in the tower of the church of St. Nicholas, the Scots' general having threatened, if the town gates were not opened, that he would batter down the steeple, in which the Newcastle people take great pride, as the chief ornament of their town. 'Tis said we shall be besieged. If it be so, and the Lord spare my life and liberty, I shall have tales to tell my Jacky which I fear he will exalt over what I read him in the profitable Holy War. Men's minds having been so agitated, business hath been at a standstill. I have been much abroad. There is talk of bringing the miners up to fight. Will the Lord spare this place? Its wickedness is great. Out of the mouths of its babes and sucklings there proceedeth not praise, but blasphemy, and cursing, and filthy talk that makes the blood run cold. 'Tis well for me I understand not all they say.

When I rebuked them, they turned upon me as though they had been men, threatening to stone me, and grown men standing near abetted them, notwithstanding the judgment which hangs over our heads. One bought from a woman a black pudding and cast it at me. Ere many days have passed, he may not be so ready to fling away his food. All classes of men, yea, and many of the women, are lamentably given up to drink. When we entered the town at five o'clock this morning the better class of tradesmen were crowding to the public-houses, and the inflamed faces which may everywhere be seen prove too plainly that drunkenness is the crying sin of this people. They who have money to buy it make a boast of the goodness of their wine. If they staved in their casks and let their beloved liquor run into the Tyne, methinks 'twould be for the betterment of their reputation. This evening the house was crowded; Mr. Wesley took for his subject Jonah's prediction of the destruction of Nineveh, insisting particularly on "Who can tell, if God will return and repent, and turn away from His fierce anger, that we perish not?" Deep awe descended on the people. God grant that the word spoken prove not unprofitable.

Thurs. 19.—To-day the Mayor hurried from the Mansion House to the Town Hall, where he called a meeting of the householders and desired as many as would to set their names to a paper, pledging themselves, at any cost to purse or person, to hold the town against the Scots.

At Mr. Wesley's desire I have again been going about the town all day, striving to speak a word in season, wherever opportunity offered. I fear with little fruit for my labour. The people mock at my southern tongue, and when I would reason with them, I comprehend not half they say—nay, sometimes not a word. When down by the riverside among the keelmen, I doubted whether I should get back alive, so rough were they in their ways. Peradventure, however, 'tis in part mere manner. 'Tis said that the soldiers are needed to keep down these keelmen full as much as to guard the town against the Scots. Amongst them who look down upon the keelmen as savages, I witnessed a most disgraceful spectacle. About one I saw a number of gentlemen assembling at a handsome house in what is called Low Friar Street, doubtless for dinner. As I passed later in the day they came staggering out, flushed with wine, and reeled off to a public house like a string of geese, to finish the day with strong ale.

Fri. 20. — The Mayor hath called the citizens to arms, and ordered the Pilgrim Street Gate to be walled up. The wall here is said to be two miles and a furlong round. 'Tis twelve feet high and eight feet thick, with towers for strengthening at the angles. At the chief entrances to the town there are towers with iron-ribbed oaken gates and portcullises. Our house being without the walls will be at the mercy of the savages in petticoats, who, 'tis said, form the main body of the Pretender's army; but the Lord will provide.

This day we have held a solemn fast, assembling for prayer at the dinner-hour, when too many of the inhabitants begin to drink away what remnant of their wit the morning drink had left them. Perchance they think thus to screw up their courage, but trust in the Lord gives surer confidence than ale and wine. It vanisheth not in the morning, like that of those who have drunk off the fumes of their overnight drink, and can bluster no more until they have maddened themselves again.

Sat. 21.—News hath come of the utter rout of General Cope's army, seasoned English soldiers scampering like hares before the wild men from the hills. The guard is doubled, and the Sally Port and the Pandon Gates have been walled up, as they were in the former rebellion in '15. Women carried the mortar and the bricks. Women here do many things which elsewhere are done by men. On what they call the Sandhill there are female barbers, who ply their trade in the open air. Mr. Wesley hath writ to the Mayor, excusing himself for his not having appeared at the Town Hall, on the ground of the smallness of his power to aid in the defence of the town, but assuring his worship of the devoted loyalty of himself and all connected with him to His Majesty King George. Mr. Wesley hath also taken occasion, believing the Mayor to be a God-fearing man, to call his attention to the frightful iniquities of this town, and to urge him to use his authority to check them in their at present unbridled riot. Mr. Wesley suffered me to read his letter before he despatched it. Methinks 'tis so worded that, if his Worship be indeed a God-fearing man, it can give no offence, but rather stir him up to put forth the power which God hath placed in his hands for the advancement of His glory. Sure, the magistrate should not bear the sword in vain, but be the minister of God for good, a revenger to execute wrath upon him that doeth evil.

Sun. 22.—The gentry dwelling within the walls are fleeing south with their goods, and in our street we shall soon be left alone, both rich and poor stripping their houses and taking their departure. Great guns are mounted on the walls, and all the guards are on the alert, an assault being hourly expected.

This morning I went with Mr. Wesley to Gateshead, which, although on the Durham side of the river, may be called a suburb of Newcastle. Houses are huddled on the battlements of the narrow bridge, and on it, moreover, there are ruins of a hermitage and a chapel. At either end there is a gateway tower with a portcullis, and another in the middle, which is used as a House of Detention for criminals. On the tower on the Northumberland side, which they call the Magazine Gate, the heads and quarters of traitors have been nailed up; as, for example, of William Wallace, one of whose quarters was here exposed upon a gibbet.

The jurisdiction of the Newcastle magistrates extending only over their portion of the bridge and river, a thief, if he can so far give their constables the slip, is free. We toiled up Bottle Bank, full as steep as what they call the Side upon the other bank of the river, and having reached an open part of the High Street, Mr. Wesley preached; hard by the Popish chapel, thus giving the Papists his defiance. Afterwards, having crossed the river, we heard an excellent sermon in St. Andrew's, the oldest church in Newcastle, still bearing marks of the Scots' siege. If all clergymen preached like that good man, there would be little need for Mr. Wesley and his preachers to go about the kingdom.

Mon. 23.—I have again been wandering in the town seeking to speak a word for Christ, but to little purpose. For now the people of Newcastle and the strangers therein spend their time in nothing else but either to tell or to hear some new thing about the rebels; and, indeed, when I open my lips about aught else, I am oft regarded with suspicion, as though I were a spy.

Tues. 24.—Another unprofitable day, causing me much dissatisfaction. O Lord, increase my faith, give me more boldness, more skill to win men's confidence. Increase of my knowledge of the town is all that I have as yet won from these my wanderings, and I came not hither for that.

Yet is the place worth a visit. Within the walls are many fair gardens and green pastures, and the houses of timber and brick, or lath and plaster, are exceeding quaint. The floors hang over one another, and there are many windows in the roofs. There is abundance of stone in the neighbourhood, and yet but one stone house in the town. Clay was even more abundant for the making of bricks; and for the building of houses, as well as ships, oak-trees grew in plenty on what they now call the Town Moor, over which the North Road runs, along which we hourly expect to see the Scots savages advancing. O Lord, be Thou our shield.

Wed. 25.—Our good friends within the walls for ever dinning in our ears, some, that if we tarry without, the wild Highland men will devour our defenceless children, and others, that the Orphan House is so placed that so soon as the town guns begin to play, 'twill be levelled with the ground, Mr. Wesley this day made a survey, and he assures me that, on the other hand, the guns are so planted that not a ball can strike us, whilst the fire from Newgate on the one side, and that from Pilgrim Street Gate on the other, would blow to pieces any who attempted to come nigh our house to do us harm. To-day he told me somewhat of his former visits to Newcastle. The colliers round about seem to be little less wild than the Scots, their children running half-naked, and the men, to show their approval of Mr. Wesley, shouting aloud in the midst of the preaching, and clapping him on the back until his breath was well-nigh gone. But the Newcastle mob, he says, hath some humanity left at its wildest. Once, being moved with compassion for the poor creatures who spent (as many still spend) their Sabbath in wandering about the Sandhill, like sheep having no shepherd, he went straight to them from church and started a psalm. Thousands soon gathered round him, but the most part spent the time in shouting and pushing; the throng heaving and tossing like a troubled sea. So after singing and praying for an hour in the midst of the tumult, he was constrained, through lack of voice, to leave them without a sermon. Nevertheless, not a stone, brickbat, rotten egg, or dead cat was thrown, nor was any other personal violence offered to him. On another occasion, during his stay in the town, the Edinburgh Company of Comedians announced the performance of a farce entitled Trick upon Trick, or Methodism Displayed. A multitude of men and women assembled to witness the performance, but, in the first act of the comedy before the farce, all the seats erected on the stage gave way with a sudden crack, and those who sat upon them were thrown headlong. The play still continuing, after order had been restored, in the second act all the shilling seats sank suddenly. This caused panic, and many forced their way out of the building in terror. But still the play went on, when lo! at the beginning of the third act, the stage itself went down six inches, the actors skipping nimbly off it in their fright. But having been persuaded by their master to return, and the piece going on, towards the end of the third act all the sixpenny seats fell without the least warning to the ground, and with loud outcries many more rushed out. Then he who was to play the Methodist, fearing that none would be left to witness his performance, came forward and affirmed that, notwithstanding all that had happened, the farce should be performed. As he spake, the stage sank six inches more, and actors and audience fled in wild confusion.

Thurs. 26.—Of the Barbican hard by they tell an idle tale, to wit, that when the clock strikes twelve at noon, the statue of the king, King James I., descends from its niche. Ah, would they think of the King of glory who shall come down in clouds to judgment! The Fighting Cocks is the sign of one of the inns here, and of that cruel and cowardly pastime this town is a headquarters. Mr. Wesley tells of a gentleman who would have come to hear him preach had he not feared he would say something against the fighting of cocks.

To-day I visited the Trinity House, in Trinity Chare, as they call here a narrow alley. The roof of the chapel is the deck of an ancient ship, or appears such. There is service there on Sunday afternoons, which, God willing, I shall attend on the coming Sabbath.

Fri. 27.—All day messengers have been spurring thick and fast with tidings that the enemy is at hand, and the number of gentry who have flocked in with their property, guarded by their servants, mounted and armed, would seem to confirm the story.

Sat. 28.—Another such day as yesterday. All men's minds in a tremor save those whose hearts are stayed on God. No sign of the enemy save fresh announcers of his coming, but the guards are doubled. The gentry still flock in from the north. One, 'tis said, the Mayor hath seized for a spy. Mr. Ridley is hot against Popery. I hear he is of the family of Bishop Ridley, who was a native of this county. O Lord, continue to watch over us. If the Lord keep not the city, the watchman waketh in vain.

Sun. 29.—'Tis confidently affirmed that the enemy will

be upon us to-morrow evening. The gentleman who was apprehended yesterday (Nixon is his name) cut his throat; but the wound was at once sewn up. This morning, Mr. Wesley preached at Gateshead, but bade me stay in Newcastle, and strive to do more good than hath hitherto fallen to my lot. He is dissatisfied with what he calls my faint-heartedness, but sure I have given proof that 'tis not fear which holds me back. Every man hath not Mr. Wesley's gift of making himself all things to all men. I feel myself, as it were, in a foreign land, and find no freedom of speech in addressing even the brethren. In the afternoon I went to the Trinity Chapel, and experienced more peace than I have yet had in Newcastle, in worshipping with the pensioners, whose worldly warfare is accomplished. God grant that they may have hope as an anchor of the soul, both sure and stedfast, and which entereth into that within the veil. Since, methinks, 'tis manifest that the Lord hath not called me to the office of a public evangelist, I would fain be back in the bosom of my family, and engaged in the humble work for the Lord which had grown familiar to me.

Mon. 30.—No sign of the rebels. Mr. Wesley hath ridden into the country to visit the societies round about.

Tues. Oct. 1.—To-day I visited the Castle, toiling up to it from the riverside by the Castle Stairs, on whose landings sellers of old shoes and clothes had pitched their stalls; and round about what they call the Castle Garth, at the top, I found shops of the same. 'Tis said this garth belongs not to Newcastle, but to the county of Northumberland, and that in former times, when none save those free of the town were allowed to trade in it, foreign cloth-sellers resorted hither, and their trade still tarries.

Wed. 2.—Mr. Wesley is returned, and with him came news that the Pretender was at last coming down upon the town in full force and by forced marches.

Thurs. 3.—This morning, before starting again for the country, Mr. Wesley told me that the brethren here (with whom backbiting would seem to be the sin which doth most easily beset them) had complained to him of my lukewarmness, inasmuch as I did not preach, but idled about the town. I answered that I had again and again striven to speak a word for Christ, but each time with worse success, and that I took this as a sign that God had not called me to be a Round preacher. He accused me of indolence, and spake as though I had proved false to the obligation under which I lay to him, through his having become answerable for the support of my family during my absence. I replied that 'twas not of my own motion I set out to travel with him; but that I would not be beholden to him for money, but would return him his bank-bill as soon as I reached my home, for which I craved his leave to depart immediately.

At this he desired me to do nothing in haste, but to tarry in the town until he likewise took his departure; at the same time asking my pardon, if he had judged me harshly. So we were reconciled; but 'tis plain he is grievously disappointed, at the which I am deeply grieved, for, methinks, I would do anything rather than wittingly wound the spirit of so good a man, so ready to condescend to them of low estate, and to own to a wrong when he thinks that he hath done one; and yet, good and great man though he be, I cannot but think that his vexation is caused in part by a consciousness that he hath erred in judgment.

After Mr. Wesley had ridden into the country, I went out into the streets and again endeavoured to proclaim the gospel of Christ; but with so stammering a tongue that I was constrained to desist through fear of wilfully casting pearls into the mire to be trodden under foot of swine. O Lord, Thou knowest 'twas not through fear that they should turn again and rend, though 'tis thus the brethren here would have it. O Lord, restore unto me Thy favour, let me again become a profitable servant in Thy vineyard. Purge my heart of bitterness, O Lord. Enable me to forgive them which have spoken evil of me, and seemed to triumph over my discomfiture. Humble my heart, O Lord. Make me willing to become nothing in the sight of men, if it be Thy will.

Fri. 4.—This day I visited the library at St. Nicholas's, and saw the old chains with which the Bibles were wont to be chained to the desk. O Lord, may I so bind Thy word unto my heart.

Tues. 8.—There now seeming little likelihood of the Pretender's coming hither, Mr. Wesley is about to set out southwards to-morrow for a time, leaving me here until his return. We have had stirring times. Last Saturday the rebels, a thousand strong, did come within seventeen miles of Newcastle. The news was not like the lying rumours by which we have been before deceived, but brought by a Newcastle burgess of repute, and accordingly the soldiers were ordered to hold themselves in readiness to march. The prisoner who cut his throat, to escape hanging as a spy, not being able to speak, made confession in writing that 'twas the Pretender's intent to seize Tynemouth Castle, and with the guns and ammunition got therefrom, to plant himself on the hill to the east of the town, and so have it at his mercy. Thereupon the Mayor sent off a messenger in hot haste to Tynemouth (they say that when he reached there his black horse might have been taken for an iron-grey, 'twas in such a lather of sweat), with orders for the securing of the munitions of war.

This evening there came from the General an officer who, ordering out Mr. Wesley as though he were a dog, bade him pull down the battlements of the house, or the General would do it for him. Mr. Wesley sent back answer in writing that he was willing to pull down not the battlements only, but the whole house, for the service of His majesty; but complained with justice of the incivility of the bearer of the summons.

Wed. 9.—This morning I went with Mr. Wesley as far as Gateshead, where he preached at four; and then, bidding him farewell for a season, went back to Newcastle to await his return. The place seems to me more than ever like a foreign land now that he is gone.

Sun. 13.—I preached to-day in the square of the Keelmen's Hospital, but found more comfort in talking afterwards with some of the old men. Age and infirmity have tamed their wildness, and one with whom I prayed, and who afterwards prayed for me, seems to be an Israelite indeed.

Wed. 16.—The number of hogs' puddings devoured in this town is prodigious. Sure, 'tis not food for one who believes his Bible. "But flesh with the life thereof, which is the blood thereof, ye shall not eat." But when I spake of this to one of the brethren, he accused me of straining at a gnat and swallowing a camel, of censoriously finding fault with an honest man for eating a "nice fat black pudden, smoken het" (as he called it), honestly paid for, whilst I dishonestly ate the bread of idleness. Were I to consult the flesh, I should oft take horse at once and return home; but I must keep my promise to Mr. Wesley, and tarry till he come. The strange manner of speech of the people here makes it hard at times to believe that they be Englishmen. Especially uncouth is what they call their bur. 'Tis as though their tongues were too large for their mouths, or they had filled them, before speaking, with their black pudding.

Tues. 22.—Mr. Wesley came back this evening, and began to preach almost as soon as he was off his horse. Although small of stature, he is a man of iron frame. Doubtless, 'tis temperance of living hath given it him. 'Tis astonishing the small amount of food he takes; attributing it to habit; because, when a young boy at the Charterhouse, the bigger boys regularly robbed him of his meat, leaving him only enough of his bread to keep life in him. He loves his old school, and makes occasions to visit it; but if this be the way in which schools for the gentry are carried on, thankful am I that my Jack is not like to be put to one of them. Methinks I witness the indignation of the little Susan at hearing that bigger boys had robbed her brother of his food. O Lord, watch over my dear family. May we soon meet in health and strength and peace.

Mr. Wesley tells me that he was stopped at Ferrybridge, and all his letters read by the general in command there. They will still have it we are in league with the Pretender. He hath visited Epworth, and given them there his Jonah sermon. Leeds hath forgotten the Duke of Tuscany, and suffered him to preach in peace. At Sheffield the preaching place was thronged, and many could not get within earshot of the sermon.

Sun. 27.—Mr. Wesley hath received an answer to the letter he wrote the Mayor, touching his willingness to preach to the poor soldiers here, if those who were paid for it would not care for their souls. Their profligacy and profaneness is appalling, and Mr. Wesley says he found the like at Doncaster. In his letter, Mr. Wesley instanced the case of John Haime and others, to show that religion makes a man none the worse a soldier, and invited the officers also to hear him, if they feared he would teach their men disloyalty. His Worship says he will lay the request before the General.

Thur. 31.—To-day Mr. Wesley preached to the English soldiers encamped on the Town Moor : " Ho, every one that thirsteth" was his text, and at first the poor stupid wretches looked up as if they thought he was promising to treat them to strong drink; but soon, though they continued as quiet, they became as insensible as logs.

Mr. Wesley confesses that John Haime would have spoken to them to better purpose. Methinks my little Jacky would lose his reverence for soldiers if he saw what manner of men they be. One of the brethren, who never loses an opportunity of setting Mr. Wesley against me, asked him why he did not send me to preach to the Germans, since I gave myself out to be too great a "scholard" to be able to preach to English folk. For this Mr. Wesley sharply rebuked him, saying that he felt full sure I had been guilty of no such presumption. 'Tis strange so good a man, being admitted by all judges to be a scholar of more than ordinary erudition, and having so many better titles to claim men's respect, should value himself so jealously as he doth on his having received a learned education.

Sun. Nov. 3.—On Friday, yesterday, and to-day, Mr. Wesley hath preached to the soldiers, the rain having been twice stayed by the good hand of God. Let those scoff at the interposition of Providence who will, the fact remains. It rained until Mr. Wesley began to speak, and began to rain again as soon as he had finished. The men, and many of their officers likewise, at last listened with great attention. There was no disturbance save on the part of one officer, and he, being ashamed of himself, to make amends when the sermon was over, took Mr. Wesley's place, and was graciously pleased to inform his men, as plain as he could speak, that what they had heard was very good. I heard a wag among them say, that the prayers were none the better for the Amen; and, indeed, the poor foolish young man was far gone in drink. He nigh tripped himself with his sword when he mounted to make his oration, which came to an end very sudden. This evening Mr. Wesley spoke in their own tongue to some of the Germans, who listened to him gladly. He tells me that though 'tis long since he used the German, it came back upon him with a rush when he saw them straining their ears and their understanding, if so they might catch something, however little, for their profit, as he spake to the English soldiers.

LEEDS, *Tues.* 5.—'Twas with dry eyes I yesterday rode out of Newcastle, having small desire to visit it again. 'Tis a place in which I endured many humiliations. The Lord make them profitable to my soul. On our road hither we met expresses, spattered with mud, spurring their horses, though already at full stretch. They scarce drew rein to tell us they were sent to stop the army's march into Scotland, for that the enemy had crossed the Tweed, and were pouring southwards, with intent to take London by surprise. When we entered, the town was ablaze with bonfires, and the streets filled with people leaping and shouting and drinking destruction to the Pope. Some of the bonfires are still alight; but the streets are very quiet, nigh deserted, Mr. Wesley having sent me to the magistrates with word of what we had heard upon the way. O Lord, watch over my dear family, and may they have a more peaceful night than we spent this time twelvemonth.

BIRMINGHAM, *Mon.* 11.—When I left Leeds, the town was still in great fear. The cloth-buyers whispering their bids to the clothiers in the market were scarce more quiet than the bulk of the people stirring. Mr. Wesley having desired me to await his coming in this town, I rid on and arrived here without accident. To-day Mr. Wesley arrived and preached. He hath been journeying in Cheshire and Stafford, hearing on his way that he was with the Pretender in Edinburgh. He tells me that he was oft stopped by wise watchmen in villages, standing sentry against the Pretender's army with their staves and blunderbusses. Some such I saw in my ride through Derbyshire; but, being a plain man, they suffered me to pass with little question. At Wednesbury his horse stuck fast in the mire after dark, and there Mr. Wesley had to sit upon its back until some came with lanterns. Whilst waiting for him, thinking it no sin to be about my worldly master's business, so long as I neglect not my heavenly Father's, I have taken knowledge of the leather trade of this town, Mr. Saunders being desirous to deal in that likewise. We are bidden to be diligent in business, but God grant that he become not careful and troubled about many things, to the neglect of the one thing needful. May he choose that good part which shall not be taken away from him. I look forward to serving him once more. He hath faults (from which who is free?), but he hath ever treated me with respect, and his dear wife with exceeding kindness.

To-morrow we part, Mr. Wesley setting out for London, and myself for my beloved home. He no longer upbraids me with having looked back after putting my hand to the gospel plough; but 'tis plain that his affection for me hath cooled. The Lord knoweth that my love and, in great measure, my reverence for him continue the same. May he still remember me and my dear family in his prayers.

XVI.

Thurs. Nov. 14.

RENDER unto Thee my hearty thanks, O Lord, for Thy goodness in restoring me to my home, where I have been received with much duty and affection. I cannot but think that in this my return I have followed the leadings of Providence. 'Twas manifest, methinks, from my failure that 'twas not the will of my Father I should engage in the public work, but rather labour in my intervals of leisure from worldly toil among them of my own neighbourhood.

Some gibe as though I had been dismissed from his service by Mr. Wesley in disgrace; and others spread the idle tale, that after joining the Pretender's army, I have fled from it through fear, having in my first battle obtained my bellyful of fighting.

This, it seems, is the Vicar's story, who talks big, 'tis said, of seizing and giving me up to the Government for a rebel. My running away, he saith, in order that he may put me to shame, doth but prove that I am a coward.

Howsoever, these slanders I regard not. By them of mine own household I have been welcomed as one given back to them from the dead. May the Lord, who I believe hath restored me to my home, graciously enable me to lead my beloved family to a knowledge of the truth.

But the things that make for their peace, alas! still they will not understand, though all else I have to tell them they drink in with greedy ears. Little Jack never wearies in hearing of the soldiers and the great guns on the walls.

Mon. 18.—When I returned to my work at Mr. Saunders's this morning, his good wife told me that to her great joy, and verily to mine likewise, poor Teddy had returned. On her way to the evening preaching yesterday, she met with him, made him prisoner by her gentleness, and afterwards made his peace with his master, and restored him to the household. His enemy, the porter, having during my absence been turned away for drunkenness and theft, I trust the poor lad may now become a steady servant. He hath been a wanderer ever since he left us, taking ship at Bristol, and crossing the sea to Waterford in Ireland, and thence to Dublin. From

Dublin he came again to Bristol, sailing thence in another vessel to a place in Wales, where, weary of the hardships of the life, and the exceeding wickedness of his companions, he left the sea. Since then, as the saying goes, he hath lived from hand to mouth, working when a job was to be got, but being at times constrained to beg for a dry crust. At length, of no intent he knows of, but doubtless led of God, he drew down nearer to his home, and providentially fell in with Mistress Saunders. Doubtless his late hardships will lead him now to put a higher price upon a peaceful home. I am thankful to say that notwithstanding the vile companionship into which he hath been thrown, he would still fain be one of Christ's disciples.

His blind father showed no pleasure when I told him of his son's return, but called him sneak and milksop for slinking back like a beaten hound creeping to heel.

Not such is his Father in heaven, who, when he was yet a great way off, had compassion on him. "There is joy in the presence of the angels of God over one sinner that repenteth." Ah, would that I could find my lost piece of silver, my lamb astray in the wilderness, my beloved Patty!

Sun. 24.—O Lord, watch over us. We have none other guide and guard to flee to. In whom else would we trust? News comes that the rebels are marching southwards fast, and that ten thousand Frenchmen have landed in Suffolk, and are hurrying to join them.

Wed. Dec. 18.—FAST DAY.—This hath been a solemn day. The church bells rang, as it were, with a warning voice. Neither here nor in Bath have I before seen so general a countenance of awe. The church was filled, and many who have hitherto held aloof from us, or openly mocked us, came to our services. O Lord, shouldest Thou in Thy mercy put forth Thy right hand, mighty to save, on our behalf, grant that the dread which now weighs upon men's minds may not pass away until many have been brought to consider their latter end, to cry with strong groanings and tears, "What must I do to be saved?"

1746—*Jan.* 1.— The Lord hath been graciously pleased to hear and answer prayer. For some days past a precious work of grace hath been carried on in our midst, and we have had some marvellous conversions. As it was said of old, "Is Saul also among the prophets?" so may we say, "Is Joyce also among the Methodists?" and joyfully answer, "Yea, thanks be unto the Lord."

He came, not persuaded by his good man, but to accompany his drunken comrade, Tom Rogers, the mason, into one of our meetings, at a time when many were pricked to the heart.

As he watched them curiously, suddenly he exclaimed at the top of his voice, "I can't stand this, Tom. If I stay here, willy nilly, I shall be converted too!" and so saying, he seized his hat, rushed out and ran home, bidding Tom follow. But the mason stood stock still, and soon, falling on his knees, began to cry aloud for mercy.

At home Joyce could not rest, but walked the roads all night. When he got back in the morning, his good man was standing at the door of the forge waiting for the key, and when they had gone in, and Joyce was furiously blowing up the fire, the man, seeing that something was amiss with his master, proposed a word of prayer. At this Joyce began to curse and swear, and flung out, vowing that none should convert him against his will. He went to the Blue Boar, where he drank madly, and some coming in who began to jest with him, telling him 'twas vain to strive, converted he must be, he flew upon them, smiting, biting, and kicking, and smashing chairs and tables in his rage, so that the landlord and his man were constrained to put him out of the house.

They led him home, and after awhile prevailed upon him to go to bed: but scarce were they gone before he rushed out again, crying aloud, so that the children of the village ran after him in wonder. 'Twas to Tom Rogers's he went, and asked him what he would have him do. That unhappy man, who had been striving to drown in drink his convictions of the night before, advised him to go back with him to the Dog and Pheasant, where he promised he would stand a gallon.

But the blacksmith's good man, who had followed his master, persuaded him to come to me, and we both prayed with him. I put off my departure to Bath for half-an-hour that I might tarry with him longer. It seemed strange to me that after I had told him the cause, Mr. Saunders should still express displeasure at my late arrival.

On my return Joyce's man came to me, praying me to go to the forge. "I believe," says he, "master might now find peace, but the devil holds him back by his pride,—he is too proud to be converted by his servant's prayers."

Accordingly I went and prayed with Joyce. Glory be to God, he soon heard the voice of mercy. Hitherto he hath walked worthy of his profession, and is striving to bring Rogers and others of his ungodly companions into the ways of righteousness and paths of peace.

Thurs. 2.—This morning on my walk into the city, I

had some talk with a carrier driving a string of packhorses. I thought at first that I had fallen into the society of a child of God, but alas! from what he afterwards let fall, I found that he had not charity, that his pious talk was empty as the jingle of his leader's bells,—a sounding brass and tinkling cymbal.

Sun. 5.—At church this morning the Bishop was present; and the Vicar, wishing, doubtless, to curry favour with his lordship, gave us a sermon against Methodism. We were fools, hypocrites, devils, rogues, all marked with the sign of the beast, reserved for everlasting burning. During the sermon I observed the face of his lordship expressing great disquiet, and in the vestry, I hear, he chid the Vicar, even before the clerk, bidding him never again presume to preach in his presence in the like foolish and uncharitable strain, under penalty of his severe displeasure.

Mon. 6.—Alas! how true is that scripture, "The heart is deceitful above all things, and desperately wicked." Two of my master's 'prentices, whom I had thought honest lads as one might find, have long fallen into the cursed practice of gaming, letting themselves down at night into the back-yard by a ladder of ropes in order to get to the gaming table. Hitherto they have supplied their needs by purloining goods from the shop and warehouses, and selling the same at a loss to rogues who have encouraged them in their dishonesty. But standing in need of larger supplies, and emboldened by impunity, they had laid a plan to rob my till in such manner that the suspicion must needs fall on the canting old Methodist, as it seems they have been in the use of calling mé, notwithstanding their reverent eyeservice. 'Twas through tampering with Ted Joyce, whom they would have had a sharer in their plot, their wickedness was brought to light. O Lord, I thank Thee for preserving my good name, which they, with no provocation (for I have ever shown them fatherly kindness), would so wantonly have slurred. O Lord, may they be saved from the gallows and hell fire.

Tues. 14.—Coming home in the dark this evening, I was knocked down by a runaway horse; but, so graciously doth the Lord watch over His servants with unslumbering eye, I fell in the bottom of the ditch, which the rain hath turned to mud softer than a feather-bed, and beyond wet clothes and a little bruise upon my shoulder, received no harm.

Wed. 15.—This day I rode to Kingswood on my master's business. Wondrous is the work which God hath wrought there by the hand of His servants, but methinks, although, in spite of the black pit mounds, it must be a fair country when the leaves are out, 'tis still the wildest part of the kingdom. The colliers seemed to me of a fiercer nature than the pitmen I saw in the North. They scowled at me as if they would fain stab me with the iron candlesticks they carry stuck like daggers through their leather hatbands; and the lads hunted and hooted me through the winding lanes as though I had been a mad dog; nay, in the place they call Cock Road, three men made attempt to stop and rob me in broad daylight. 'Tis strange the men should be so savage, inasmuch as the women who come to Bath market from Kingswood with their eggs and apples would seem to be of a kindly disposition.

The school stands in the middle of the wood. They showed me the sycamore under which Mr. Wesley takes his stand. Wild though the place seems, nigh upon a hundred of the brethren and sisters have walked through the snow from Kingswood to attend the Bristol lovefeasts, going back in a body for their better protection.

Wed. April 2.—Mr. Wesley hath visited us, and appeased the contentions which had again begun to trouble our Society. I esteemed it a great privilege to be again permitted to see him face to face, to profit by his counsel, and be remembered in his prayers; although his manner towards me be not so warmly loving as of old. 'Tis plain he thinks me guilty of lukewarmness; nay, he told me openly, he feared 'twas my example had proved a stone of stumbling to my family. I pray this be not true,—even the best of men may err; but if it be, may God forgive me, and stir me up to greater earnestness.

Mr. Wesley told me of our brethren in Flanders. Brother Clements was shot through both arms in battle, and three others slain; so that Brother Haime was left alone, of the little band of believers.

Mon. 7.—To-day I was at Kingswood, where Mr. Wesley laid the first stone of the New House, a great crowd listening thirstily as he opened to them this scripture: "For brass I will bring gold," &c. May the prophecy be indeed fulfilled at Kingswood: "Violence shall no more be heard in thy land, wasting nor destruction within thy borders; but thou shalt call thy walls and thy gates Praise." As I guessed, 'tis a fair country now that the spring is come. The elm trees are in leaf and the black-thorn is out in abundant blossom. About the cottages likewise, the fruit trees have begun to flower. 'Tis strange to see the black-faced colliers coming out of their white cottages in their grimy clothes. I rode with Mr. Wesley and a friend in the evening as far as Bath, where controversy ensued between Mr. Wesley and my master. He will not but have it that Mr. Saunders hath, by raising my wage for his own profit, tempted me from the preaching of the Gospel. It grieves me to see that good Mistress Saunders, although she will not allow that her husband hath erred, seemeth to think that I have been in some way in the wrong. I love not controversy; 'twas sweeter this morning to hear the birds singing in the woods, and the colliers joining in the psalms.

Tues. May 6.—To-day I read carefully the rules which Mr. Wesley drew up for the first Society in Fetter Lane. Doubtless they approve themselves to an enlightened judgment in the gross; but here, at least, methinks, objection might be taken to some.

We are again, I thank the Lord, at peace; and I pray it may continue. But we have more than once been disturbed, and at times, had the eleventh rule been enforced, seeing that most had been set against me, I might have been shut out from the Society by those whom I had, under God, brought into it. Since my return from the North, especially since it hath been seen that Mr. Wesley no longer holds me in the high esteem wherewith he once honoured me, I have noticed an increasing wish to make little of my words. Ah, had some of the sisters here the humble mind and willingness to learn of that poor negro woman, of whom Mr. Wesley tells, in the Plantations, 'twould be well for their growth in grace. And, peradventure, it were well if some of our brethren more often meditated on those profitable scriptures, " Be not high-minded, but fear," " Heady, high-minded, having a form of godliness, but denying the power thereof." Oh, may I never fall into the snare of thinking of myself more highly than I ought, and despising others, like those poor ignorant men.

XVII.

LONDON, *Thurs. June* 12.

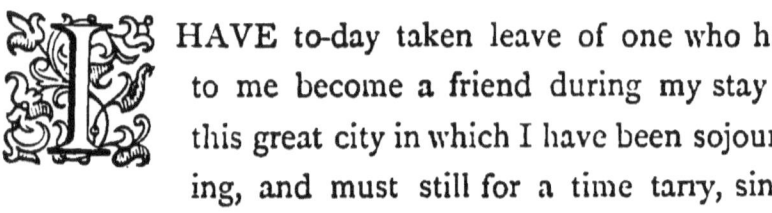 HAVE to-day taken leave of one who had to me become a friend during my stay in this great city in which I have been sojourning, and must still for a time tarry, since my master's business is not yet finished. Methinks the lawyers spin out the time and spread their paper for mere love of lucre; and that the London accountants are slow of purpose. Had it not been for my dear friend, Sampson Staniforth, my time here had not been a season of refreshing; inasmuch as, since Mr. Wesley no longer regards me with favour, most of the Society here look upon me as a worldling. But in Sampson I have found a familiar friend; I met him at the Foundery, whither he had come from Deptford. This day I have parted from him there; he on his very wedding day having been commanded to join his regiment, under orders to embark at Gravesend for Holland.

He is a Yorkshireman, and was bred a baker; but falling into bad company, listed when drunk. His mother bought him off; but being sent out with bread, he got one to carry back his basket to his master, and again listed. At first the regiment lay at Edinburgh,—their bedding being dirty straw in the castle vault; and, spending his money on his lusts, Sampson, between pay days, oft wanted food. At Glasgow he heard Mr. Whitefield; but his words were to him but as the idle wind. At a place called Ayr he was nigh drowned when drunk with others in a boat at sea. At Perth, Highland soldiers would have slain him for proving false to his promise to marry a countrywoman, had he not been warned in time by the poor girl he had deserted. At that time he was altogether given up to the devil and his works. In Flanders he led the same wicked life. But a comrade who had found peace after attending the preaching of Mr. John Haime, and his friends, took him in hand, and ere long he was convinced of sin. He had no Bible, but his friend gave him a bit of an old one, and thenceforth no persuasion or ridicule from his dissolute companions could lead him shamefully to plunder (although at the risk of being shot or hanged) the poor inhabitants of the country, or to indulge in any other of the vices in which he had before shamelessly revelled. His comrade, clubbing his own pay with his, helped him at much sacrifice to pay his debts; and the change in his behaviour, and his own and his friend's exhortations, led others to amend their lives. But still the Lord had not spoken peace unto his soul; but at Ghent, while standing sentry, he heard the blessed words, "Thy sins are forgiven thee," and could scarce believe his ears when the corporal came round to say his time was up; so full was his soul of joy. But afterward he lost his raptures; nevertheless, he kept hold on Christ with a firm hand of faith. Feeling some alarm before the battle of Fontenoy, he prayed to God to enable him to quit himself like a good Christian soldier; and thenceforth felt no fear. Over him, and his friend likewise, Providence watched in the conflict. His friend was twice struck, but the one ball hit upon a coin in his pocket, and the other on a claspknife. But many of the Society were slain. The paymaster of Sampson's regiment offered to take him as his servant in the room of one killed at Fontenoy; but was not displeased when Sampson refused, because he would not cut himself off from communion with his Christian friends, or do work not of necessity upon the Sabbath.

After our defeat at Preston Pans, his regiment was hurried to Helvoetsluys to be embarked for Gravesend, whence they came, by way of Bexley, to Deptford, where, when drawn up in the Broadway, a Christian man found them out, and invited them to praise and prayer at his house. To meet the rebels, the regiment was hurried northwards; the Methodists ever inquiring for their brethren when they halted on the road. From Stafford our army marched in the frosty night to meet the rebels, who—the spies had suddenly brought in word —were not two hours off. But on the march at dawn came news that the rebels had taken the Derby road, thinking so to slip by to London.

Thereupon part of the army was hurried northwards, and part sent back to London. Sampson's regiment was of those that returned, and was quartered in Greenwich and Deptford, where it lay until April in this year, with orders that no man should stray above a mile from his billet. But Sampson obtained leave for himself and his friends to go twice or thrice a week to London, to hold communion with Mr. Wesley and the Society; the commanding officer saying that he knew Mr. Wesley well, and was glad that they had made so good a choice. At Deptford, Sampson made the acquaintance of the good woman who hath to-day become his wife.

Having once gone on an errand for one of the Society to Eltham, he was seized by a serjeant and soldiers as a deserter; but the commanding officer finding that they had no license to be there, threatened them with the guard-house, and at once released my friend.

One night as he came from the Foundery, a soldier met

him, and bade him make haste, since orders to march had come.

Accordingly the regiment marched next morning for Canterbury, and afterwards for Dover Castle. Having obtained a fortnight's furlough, he returned to Deptford, and during that time, having met him in the meetings of the Society here, I have made his acquaintance to the refreshment of my soul. The Lord grant that I may again commune with him in the flesh.

Wed. 18.—Back again, to my joy, in my own home. This evening I walked with my little Susan in the woods, where we, between us, gathered a big bowpot of flowers, among them, Star of Bethlehem, most abundant here; were it but for its name alone, 'twould be a plant pleasant to behold, and it seems a pity they should bring the spikes to market as they do, before the flowers have opened, to serve but for the pot.

Thurs. 19.—There was reported to me this morning a remarkable case of conversion, in which I can see nothing more to be put aside as incredible than in that of Eli and Samuel. As Molly Pease, of the next parish, was busy with the cows in the yard, she heard, as she thought, her mistress's voice calling her, and went back into the house. But her mistress saying, "I never called thee, wench," sent her back to her work. Scarce was she on her stool, before she heard the voice again, and ran in, saying, "Sure, mistress, you did call me." Her mistress, startled at this, replied, " Nay, Molly, if thou hear'st the voice again, come not to me, but list for what further shall be said."

Then a third time came the voice to Molly in the yard, bidding her go up into the granary and pray earnestly for the forgiveness of her sins.

Up to that time she had not known herself a sinner, but now a conviction of her need of a Saviour came upon her.

She retired to the granary, and falling on her knees, with none but the Almighty ear and the rats and mice to hear her, sought for and obtained pardon.

I saw her this evening, and to me her narrative varied not by one jot or tittle from that she had given to my informant of the morning, save that she added, that at the time God spoke peace to her soul, she heard as plainly as she had heard the calls before, these words spoken : "Neither do I condemn thee. Thy sins be forgiven, go in peace."

Thurs. July 17.—Mr. Wesley writes me that he hath at last, for the sake of becoming an ensample, resolved to give up tea, with much inconvenience, nay, pain and apparent injury to himself for three days; but having sought help from God in prayer, with none upon the fourth, or since.

In this matter only can I say that I am farther on the road than that good man. 'Tis some time back, on his representations, I relinquished the use of tea; and since I have never tasted a dish. True, 'tis little tea I ever drank. If my dear wife would give it up, 'twould be a greater trial and a greater gain. But she would think it hard if I seemed to grudge her an innocent indulgence, as she considers it; and I would not exert authority in what may be a doubtful matter. Good Mistress Saunders returns thanks to God over a dish of tea as one of His best gifts, notwithstanding her reverence for Mr. Wesley. 'Tis needless to say that my master will not hear a word said against the drinking of tea. Were all his customers to follow my example in this matter, he would lose much profit. I have heard that Mr. Whitefield at Oxford drank sage tea without sugar. When I lay at the Bell at Gloucester, the host made jest of this to me, saying, 'twas well Brother George and the Methodists had not their way, or not a cask of ale should be tapped, nor bottle broached in the kingdom. 'Twas scurvy behaviour, he said, for George to seek to stop the trade to which he had been bred.

Sun. 20.—This hath been a peaceful Sabbath. I was up before the sun, but found the lark up before me, singing his morning hymn high in the cool heavens. 'Twas no hindrance to my prayer and meditation, and a help unto my praise. At the early preaching, and again at eight, there was a larger gathering, and a more united, than we have had of late. At church, the Vicar being away, a gentle old man preached not the Gospel, indeed, but sound morality (if any morals can be sound not founded on faith in the atoning efficacy of the blood of our Lord Jesus Christ), and, instead of rancour, a spirit of good-will. He gave us no second sermon, but the evening prayers, as read by him, were more solace to my soul than ever I had found them from the Vicar's lips. The old gentleman, moreover, spake kindly to me in the churchyard, excusing himself (not, it seemed to me entirely in jest) for having preached but one sermon in the day, on the ground that he had heard I preached so many.

The preaching at five was another refreshing season, and in the Society meeting afterwards the Spirit of peace descended gently on us like the dew. 'Twas the same with my family at home. I saw not one angry look, nor heard a wrangling word.

As we sat together in the garden, shut in by the high privet hedge, over which the white bindweed bells were climbing, and smelling the sweet scent of the honeysuckle, the Sabbath would have seemed for a time a peaceful island in a troubled sea, a green resting-place in a bare wilderness, had it not been for the thought of our poor, lost wanderer therein.

XVIII.

Mon. July 21.

ON my return from business I was met with the news that my dear little lad had narrowly escaped drowning while bathing, having been tempted out of his depth, indeed, into as bad a hole as any in the river, by a wicked lad, who trod water to deceive him. I will not say that it was the intent of the rascal that my boy should drown; but he did nothing for his succour. Perchance 'twas through fright. Leaving my little boy whom he had led into danger to sink or rise, he swam to the farther bank, and watched his struggles. But, thanks to Thy never-failing providence, O Lord, the good man who saved me from a watery grave, drew nigh the place; and, plunging in, rescued my little lad. Lord, do Thou reward his deliverer, and may the life which Thou again hast spared be devoted to Thy service.

When I call to mind the many marvellous escapes

which the boy, although so young, hath had, it is borne in upon me that he is destined for some great and good work. A gun hath gone off at half cock close by his head, and yet but a single pellet grazed his ear. He hath been thrown down by a fierce dog, but when it seemed about to worry him to death, he rolled beyond the tether of its chain as if blown by a sudden wind. An ox hath run at him, and but driven its sharp horns into a fence, with Jacky safe between. Once before he hath fallen into deep water, when he was carried over a weir, and yet brought out alive. When climbing the church tower by the ivy, he fell nigh from the bell-loft window, and they who ran to pick him up expected to find nought but a breathless bag of broken bones. Nevertheless, he had received neither bruise nor scratch. O Lord, I thank Thee for Thy goodness, and again pray that he may become Thy faithful servant and soldier.

It gives me joy that though of so venturesome disposition he hath a tender heart. The little Susan, cuddling her cheek against her little cat, which looks up at her with nigh as innocent a face, is scarce gentler in her treatment of dumb animals than Jack. Ignorant parents and other foolish folk, with their silly excuses for the ways of boys (instead of chiding or chastising them into better ways), lead the children to believe it brave to torture or more mercifully kill outright any creature not able to help itself, and make them suffer in return. But 'tis cowards who are cruel, as 'tis plain to see when a baited bull breaks from the stake. Then lo! the baiters who had thought it safe to egg on the dogs change their shouts of triumph for shrieks and screams of terror, and flee, trampling down one another in their fright like mice before a cat.

Tues. 22.—To-day, being at Keynsham, I visited Samuel Brent, a true servant of the Lord, but ever living under a cloud. "Whom the Lord loveth He chasteneth." Since he was turned of forty, he hath been subject to breast-pang, which at any time may end his days. His faith is at once firm, yet feeble, and he shudders at the thought of being called suddenly before the Lord. When I went in he was in one of his fits, and I grieved to behold a face so full of pain and fear. His wife was administering his remedies, but until I went in they had profited him nothing. Straightway I knelt down and began to pray, and soon after the pain left him. Lord, what am I that Thou hast been so good unto me, while servants of Thine who are more faithful eat the bread and drink the water of affliction all their days? And yet, methinks, we should not have to stir up our gratitude by looking down on others in a manner, half-thinking in our hearts that we are more acceptable unto God than they, but receive all His benefits with thankful hearts as miserable worms. O Lord, Thou hast been very gracious unto me.

As I rode over the bridge, the smooth river was fair to behold, with the sun shining on its bosom, and the elms, and poplars, and green pastures, on either hand; but I called to mind how narrow had been the escapes from drowning of my Jacky and myself, and starting like one who hath nigh trodden on a snake, I again gave thanks unto the Lord.

N.B.—Goody Brent tells me of a strange cake they eat at Keynsham in the spring, made of the young eels which then swarm up the river in countless numbers. These they scour until white as milk, roll into balls, and fry. If, as most men think, though I do not, flesh, fish, and fowl are given for our food, great waste of it is made by this practice.

Wed. 23.—In our service on the Green, I noted that, as soon as we began to sing, the beasts on the common came from the most distant parts and gathered about us, scattering when the prayer and sermon began, but once more gathering about us at the sound of the last hymn. Doubtless this hath happened before, but I had not before noted it. On remarking upon it at home, Jack brought to my mind that the little dog Dash which the blacksmith hath given him, wherever we may be, and wherever he, always runs up, in or out, at the sound of our singing; sometimes lifting up his head and baying, as if he would fain join in the psalm. Are the brutes then as it were dumb worshippers of our common Maker? "O all ye works of the Lord, bless ye the Lord. Praise Him and magnify Him for ever." Will there ever be a time in which in reply the whole visible creation will burst forth in audible praise and thanksgiving? There may be no express Scripture warrant for the belief, but sure there is none against, that the inferior creatures have an immortal spirit and power to enjoy an hereafter, and since through no sin of their own they have shared the evils which came upon the earth through the fall of man, why may they not be permitted to share the joys of his redemption?

Sun. Aug. 3.—Ferris the carpenter came to our evening preaching. Once or twice before he hath been present, not openly to scoff, but silently to sneer. He never joined with those who persecuted us, but contented himself with looking down upon us with much amusement, as a set of madmen running about making a great stir about a dream, a bubble that would burst, and leave them staring blankly in one another's faces. Whereas, 'twas he who was the fool, since he had said in his heart, "There is no God." What was talk of a judgment to come to him who believed in no Judge, no hereafter, no soul, no Creator?

His presence had ever acted as a whetstone to my intellects, and I had set myself to show him that, on his own principles of reason, we were no such fools as he was pleased to profess to take us for. This evening my subject admitted of no such treatment, and, at the sight of Ferris, at first I thought of changing it. But I had chosen it because high-minded contentions having again broken out amongst us, I thought it needful to recall our people to an acceptance of salvation through simple faith in Christ. Might not the blood of their souls lie at my door, if I went out of my way to show my wit in very like another vain attempt to convince one obstinate, self-opinionated man? Accordingly I took the subject I had originally prepared with more than ordinary care, and, methinks, preached with more than ordinary earnestness.

I gave little thought to Ferris, but when my eye chanced to fall upon him, to my astonishment I found him listening, not with quiet scorn, but with deep attention. When the service was finished, he would have tarried to speak with me, but I bade him come to my house when the Society meeting was over. As soon as we met, he said, " Mr. Pidgeon, I am glad you attempted not to-night to prove to me there is a God. My faith in Him is now as firm as your own. I am no longer an atheist. More, I would be a Christian. You spake to-night of coming to

Christ, but spake for those who had already known the way. I am young on the road, and would fain have farther guidance." We communed together for at least an hour; then he gladly accepting my offer, I prayed for him; and I now have good hope of his salvation.

Wed. 6.—Mr. Wesley, to whom one of the false brethren hath sent complaints of my lukewarmness, worldly-mindedness, and nevertheless desire to domineer in spiritual matters over those who walk with God more closely than myself, hath writ me a letter, not of rebuke (for that he is too just until he have heard both sides), but desiring me to give an account of myself. I fear from its tone that that good man, whose favour 'tis plain I have, to my heartfelt sorrow, forfeited, is disposed to think these charges true. I have returned this reply:—

"REV. AND HONOURED SIR,—Whatever your opinion be of me, through life, through all eternity, I shall look upon you with love and reverence, for 'twas through you that I was brought to Christ. My personal communion with you I shall hold my greatest spiritual privilege not direct from the hand of God; and though of late, when I have been honoured with admittance to your company, your words have at times been bitter—these rebukes, doubtless, have been for the good of my soul. So with gratitude I have taken and so found them.

"But for these accusations which mine enemies bring against me, may I, dear and honoured Sir, with deep respect ask why (as I fear to be the case) you are inclined to believe them well founded?

"The Lord working by the meanest of His servants, 'twas through me that Methodism was introduced into this village, and, methinks, the least friendly of my accusers cannot charge me with lukewarmness in the earlier period of my labours. Since then open persecution hath ceased here (perchance only for a time, and were it to return, it might prove a fan to winnow the chaff from the grain), but I have not slackened in my labours, save during my sickness, and my absence with you, at your bidding, in the North, and for a short while after the loss of my dear child. And though there hath not been here, peradventure, through contentiousness and lack of prayer, any general outpouring of the Spirit such as we have known, yet still do I not lack seals to my ministry.

"For worldly-mindedness, if it be worldly-minded to work faithfully in my worldly work (to which methinks Providence hath called me, not alone for worldly honour, but that so I may have more leisure and opportunities to do the more special work of the Lord), then am I worldly-minded; but, methinks, I thus act more honestly than had I gone about preaching the Gospel at other folks' charges, when I found not myself specially called to the work. Perchance, if some of my accusers were worldly-minded in like manner, their families and the cause of God would have reason to rejoice thereat.

"For desire to domineer, you, Sir, appointed me for a Class Leader, and would not excuse me from undertaking that office. If it be your pleasure to appoint another Leader over my head, I will regularly listen to his instructions. If you forbid me to preach, I will, at any sacrifice, obey, striving to believe that to you, and not to mine own heart, the Lord hath spoken.

"With love and reverence, which change elsewhere will not cause to wax cold, I shall ever remain, Reverend and Honoured Sir, your humble and attached servant (and I trust the Lord's),

"NATHANIEL PIDGEON."

What I have written, I have written, and will stand by.

Fri. 15.—To-day our dear Hester hath left us to be own maid to Lady D——, by Glo'ster. I could have been well content to keep the dear child at home, until she found one of her own. Nay, but for her happiness, it would have well pleased me had she never left me. I have no desire to part with my daughters, either to husbands or to service. Of one I have been bereaved. My wife says, "It is time the child made her own living," and when I say that she well earns her keep, affirms that she ought to have more wage than I can give her. Sarah is never at loss for a last word.

But for her mother, Hetty, methinks, would have small desire to leave her home. She hath been much sobered ever since she hath been convinced by our poor Patty's silence that her sister must be dead, if she have not come to shame instead of advancement. I believe that the Lord is secretly working on my Hester's heart. She should not leave me, but that Lady D——'s household is small and sedate, and her ladyship one of the few of the great ones of this world who have set their faces Zionwards. My master's business calling me at times to Glo'ster, I can see my child. My wife speaks much of the worldly advantage it will be to her to be about my lady's person: for this I care little; but I trust that her ladyship's companionship and counsel may be of profit to my daughter's immortal soul.

Sun. 17.—It is not often his Reverence unbends to speak with me, but meeting me this evening on my way to our preaching, he would fain have stopped me, not as was his wont, by bullying words, but by an argument. 'Twas sin, he said, for me to preach, inasmuch as I was not a successor of the apostles. Methinks the foolish young man would find it a task beyond his power to prove himself one in any manner. The argument he finished with was to send a fool to our service, who first strove to stare me out of countenance, and, failing, next sought to put me out of countenance with grimaces, meanwhile stopping his ears. Again was he discomfited, and casting a look of anger upon me, rose and went upon his way, with as much noise as his heavy heels could make. This opportunity which he hath neglected of hearing the gospel may be his last. "He that hath ears to hear, let him hear." I endeavoured to preach as a dying man to dying men. The thought of death hath been much upon my mind. In the churchyard to-day I spied a corner in which I would fain be buried with my family if we tarry in this place. Mr. Wesley tells me that the Moravians, in their ground at Hernhuth, bury separately their married men and married women, their widows, spinsters, bachelors, and male and female children. But I love not such divisions. Sure families will not be sundered thus in heaven.

Sat. 23.—I have been on my master's cheese business to the Mendips. At Chedder, I went into one of the caves: most curious; the water which soaks through the roof leaving the earth it hath taken up as rock in pillars and fantastic shapes, which I am assured are natural, though they appear the work of a chisel, cut by a carver of quaint design. Some, that hang from the roof like candles, dripping on others that are growing up from the ground to join them, ring like bells when they are struck.

They showed me water which flows underground from a place they call Wookey Hole, six miles off, into which, if you throw a dead dog, it comes out at Chedder. Thus are our hidden sins brought to light. At Glastonbury, where they say Joseph of Arimathea's staff took root, and budded like Aaron's (save that it became a tree), and tell many idle tales of St. Dunstan—I visited what is left of the Abbey, which it is plain must have been a building exceeding fine. The kitchen hath four fireplaces, named after the four evangelists, at each of which an ox might have been roasted whole. The last abbot, it is said, was hanged upon a tower upon a hill, to the top of which I climbed, the lookout therefrom being exceeding wide, beyond the Bristol Channel. Wearyall Hill they call the hill where Joseph of Arimathea rested on his thorn staff. Mr. Saunders is well satisfied with what I have done. Peradventure he will one day give me a small share of his business, and sure it is better to be a shopkeeper, prospering honestly, and thus able to advance the work of the Lord by gifts as well as my labours in my leisure hours, than to take poor pay for the regular preaching of the gospel, a work to which I do not find the Lord hath called me.

Sun. 24.—John Bunce from Bristol was here to-day, —a hearty, honest man, and, methinks, a sincere Christian. He assured me that during a voyage from the

West Indies he beheld the kraken, or sea serpent, heaving nigh a mile upon the sea. I cannot but believe him. Did he tell me anything else, should I not give him credit? and what do men find so marvellous in a creature a mile long inhabiting the mighty sea? Sure it hath room and to spare for hosts of huger monsters. It seems to me presumptuous for them who have ever tarried on dry land to declare that there is no such thing because they have not seen it brought to shore, making them out to be liars who affirm they have beheld it with their own eyes, honest master mariners whose word, even in matters of money, would be considered as good as their bond. "They that go down to the sea in ships, that do business in great waters; these see the works of the Lord, and His wonders in the deep." John tells me that Mr. Wesley is at Bristol, on his return from Wales. He spake, John says, when he told him that he should see me on the morrow, not slightingly, but sadly of me, as one who, he feared, had left my first love, and fallen from the first works through being puffed up with vain conceit of myself, being wise in my own eyes. O Lord, grant that it be not so. Let not my candlestick be removed out of his place.

Thurs. Sept. 4.—I have seen my dear Hetty more than once during my stay at Glo'ster, Lady D—— suffering me to visit her house, and in her complaisance, as I lay not at an inn, but at a private lodging, permitting my child to come into the city, and spend the better part of a day there with me. I thank the Lord not only for His goodness in keeping her in health, and giving her a merciful mistress, but for the work He hath wrought upon her soul.. She cannot yet with full confidence claim Christ as her Saviour, but 'tis plain that the Lord is fast drawing her to Himself. Oh, how I yearn for the ingathering of the first fruits of my family. Then a secret voice encourages me to hope I may look forward to an abundant harvest. God grant that not a sheaf be left behind. Lady D—— gives me accounts of my daughter's sobriety of behaviour which are most satisfactory to my mind. Her ladyship adds that in her household, wherein all are of middle age, and God-fearing folk, she hath little temptation to act otherwise; but, with deference, I have observed that the young who have not the root of the matter in them, are the more inclined to fly out into frivolity, as it were from contrariety and desire to throw off a yoke, by strictness of their elders.

Hetty reads much to her mistress. Her ladyship was pleased to praise me for having taught my child not only to pronounce her words with remarkable propriety for a girl so bred, and without gabbling, but also with due emphasis, so that she reads with understanding. Her ladyship appears a woman of much intelligence. She is not of so great estate as my wife believed, and sees but little company; but I would not have it otherwise, for Hetty's sake. Her ladyship's fine kinsfolk keep away from her, because her words and ways are too sober for their tastes. She has but a pony-chair. Her mansion ('tis a jointure house) is but such a homestead as I might look forward to spend my old age in, if God prosper me in trade. But though neither great nor grand, 'tis full of comfort, looking out beyond the forecourt (well filled with shrubs) on the village street, and the church hard by; and behind on a flower-garden with a lawn, on which stands a sun-dial, summer-houses, and a small fish-pond, in the middle of which a fountain may be made to play; a walled kitchen garden, a well-stocked orchard, and a paddock for her ladyship's cows and poultry.

When my daughter passed the day with me, I went with her to the cathedral. Indeed, before I had not been myself inside. 'Tis a grand building, of which the columns are exceeding fine; but is the Gospel preached within its walls? We saw likewise the place where Bishop Hooper was burnt, in St. Mary's Square. By the City Cross a broken soldier with a wooden leg was begging. Hetty telling me when we had passed that 'twas Patty's forsaken lover (Edward Frith, as I have found his name to be), I went back, not thinking he would know me. He took my alms and answered to my inquiry, indifferent enough, that he had lost his leg in the late wars, like many a better man and a worse. But then, looking up, the poor drunken wretch began to curse and swear at me by name at a frightful rate, and heaped such vile names on my poor child for the plight into which she had brought him, that I was constrained to turn upon my heel, having lost for the time even my wish to help him. Whatever she may have done, no woman in poor Patty's place can force a man to do wrong, unless he incline of himself to listen to the evil one.

Yet must I, for her sake, seek him out. Nay, ought I not to take pity on him as a sinner lost to all eternity if Christ save not?

Fri. 5.—There hath been a wonderful display of God's power to save and to destroy at the Quarries. Brother Sam Sturt, the only godly man at Dolland's, was taking his dinner in the shade of a ledge of rock, with two of his fellow workmen on the one side, and three upon the other, all five of notorious loose lives, bad among the bad, nay, worst among the worst. Suddenly the rock gave way, but, splitting in sunder as it fell, our dear brother escaped unharmed, while, on the other hand, the two fragments crushed the breath, yea, the very shape, out of the five. Oh, when will sinners consider?

Sat. 6.—Going out from the shop to-day to my dinner, I heard a shout of "Mad dog!" from many behind, chasing it, while those in front scattered right and left, striving to run into doors and entries. I for myself sought shelter, but chancing to see that one of the runners was Mistress Saunders, and that the dog was fast gaining on her, I prayed to God for strength, and sallying out, seized hold upon a stone and hurled it at the beast's head with so sure an aim and so strong a force that it knocked him over and dashed out his brains as his teeth snapped in the skirts of my master's wife. When I found that she was uninjured, how thankful I felt to the Lord for having suffered me to be instrumental in the preservation of that good woman. Nay, doubtless, my providential presence was more directly brought about.

Tho', after Paris, Bath be the politest of cities, yet hath it the roughest rabble. Cried one, "Th' old Methody hath but done it to curry favour with his master. He ud fain ztep into t'other old cheat's zhoes when he's weary o' his cheatun." "Nay," cried another, "if he wants th' old tup's zhop, he zhunna ha' zaved his wife. Thic wunna plazur un." I rejoiced that Mistress Saunders heard not their ribald talk. 'Tis strange, that mention of the shop. Hath any word got abroad of a likelihood of my master's making me partner in his business? Methinks, whatever such vile scum may say, 'twill advance me in my master's favour to have saved his wife from a death so horrible; but God knows that 'twas with no thoughts like these I ran the risk of encountering the same.

But sincerely do I rejoice that by imperilling my life on her behalf, I have recovered the favour of good Mistress Saunders, which hath been clouded towards me since, because I must obey the voice of God speaking to me by Providence and conscience, I made bold to disregard the wish, nay, nigh command, of Mr. Wesley concerning my giving myself up entirely to the work of preaching.

Sun. 7.—Alas, I fear that the devil is again among us. At the Society Meeting this evening, one, who hath never been distinguished for gifts or graces, arose confidently and announced the approaching end of the world. Nay, she had the assurance to proclaim the day—the 9th of next month. Some believe the vain young woman, for she is not so much crazy as conceited. If this prophecy led them to search their hearts, and walk more close with God, I could believe something in it, but it seems like to end in mere idle babble.

XIX.

Mon. Sept. 8.

 HAVE received to-night a letter from dear Hetty, which hath strangely moved me. She urges me to set out to her with utmost possible speed, and yet gives no reason for her urgency. For herself, she writes, she is in good case, and yet again urges me. I would she had been more explicit. I believe her not whimsical, but Mr. Saunders knows her not, and may think I ask too much in desiring to leave home again so soon on business not his own. I trust my Saturday's work may plead for me. In Mistress Saunders I shall have a friend. Go I must, at whatever cost. The child's words have stirred me with I know not what hopes and fears; I dare not write down my guesses.

Sat. 13.—O Lord, I thank Thee. Before I make entry of my late experiences, I would again record that I thank Thee with my whole heart and soul. According to my fear, I had difficulty with Mr. Saunders. When at last I reached Lady D——'s, and we were alone, poor Hetty reproached me by her look and by her tones for my late arrival.

"Oh, father," she cried, bursting into tears, "'tis my belief that Patty is in Glo'ster, and I had none but you to send to seek her."

Her words cut me to the quick. Who but a father should be first to seek his lost child?

"I could not tell my mistress," went on Hetty, sobbing, "for Patty's sake, for yours, for mamma, for all of us;" and again she broke down.

When she had recovered herself, she told me that being sent into Glo'ster on an errand for her mistress, she fell in with Frith, drunk according to his custom now, it would seem. Seeing that he knew and made to speak with her, she would have passed him, but he seized her roughly, and hissed into her ear that Patty was in Glo'ster. He boasted that her fine gentleman had turned her off, and then he swore that he would wring his neck; adding circumstances of vileness to my poor child's fall, which, thanks be unto the Lord, have proved to be mere lies. I pray they may be lies of madness. Did I think them lies of malice, I would not answer for myself. In any case, the wretch must now run his course unhelped for me. Even in madness, to conceive such thoughts of a woman whom he had made believe to love! After speaking with my daughter, I made search for the fellow. When I had found him, he led me, willing enough, to a house in a mean part of the city, in which he said my Patty lodged. I offered him money, which he refused, drunkard though he be, saying with a short, bitter laugh that he would be paid for his pains by the thought of what I should behold.

As I went up the cramped, creaking stairs, I heard a woman's voice, not of upbraiding, and yet there sounded reproach in its pleading. She was saying that she herself was a poor woman, and that tho' she would not press for money owing, she must needs have the chamber free to let again, so that she might pay her way. Then one strove to answer proudly. Before it broke in sobs, I knew the voice. Past the landlady I ran up into the room. 'Twas as I knew, my Patty. At sight of me she threw up her arms, and, without a cry, swooned upon the floor. Her landlady, whose small claims were easily discharged, appeared sincerely grieved at my daughter's plight, and to feel for me in my distress. She gave good account of poor Patty's behaviour during her sojourn in the house, since her desertion, shortly before the birth of the dead babe. I thank the Lord for having taken it, but poor Patty sorely mourns its loss.

When I had gotten the dear child to mine inn, I sent

for Hetty, and 'twould have moved a heart of stone to witness the meeting of the sisters.

At home, too, our poor wanderer was lovingly welcomed by the children, tho' with a certain strangeness. 'Twas different with her mother. She who most encouraged the poor lass in her folly, is hardest in judgment on its fruits.

O Lord, again I thank thee on my bended knees, and with a grateful heart, for Thy goodness in restoring her unto us. It is meet that we should make merry and be glad, for the lost is found.

Sun. 14.—Instead of a rest, this hath been a troubled day. My wife hath spoken harshly because of Patty's wish to keep the house instead of going abroad so soon after her return home. Sure, 'tis natural, and a mother should be willing to screen her child. My wife says that 'tis her wont to begin as she means to go on, and that we cannot afford to keep the girl mewed up like a grand sick lady. If she hath sinned, let her bear the shame. But in this matter 'tis my intent to put forth my authority. Patty hath no desire to be burdensome to us, but to maintain herself by work at home with her needle, and I will see that she obtain it. Oh, may the Lord speak peace to her wounded heart, so that some measure of her wonted mirth may return! 'Tis sad to note my child, once gay as any singing-bird and as active, moping still and mute in corners.

Mon. 15.—I heard in Bath to-day that good old Sister Wildash is dead. She took in a starving beggar woman and caught the fever, which the poor wretch had unconsciously upon her. Doubtlessly, our dear sister will hear the "Well done, thou good and faithful servant. Inasmuch as ye did it unto one of the least of these My servants, ye have done it unto *Me*."

Tues. 16.—To-day I dined at my master's table, a Presbyterian gentleman being present. He would have had it that 'twas wrong to kneel at prayers in public worship, but being challenged to show 'twas unscriptural, he failed. Then said he, "But call you it kneeling to sit down on the seat, and crook the back forward to the book-desk? Sure, 'twere better to do one thing or t'other." Doubtless herein he is right, save in the case of them which are too infirm to kneel, a posture which to some brings faintness.

Wed. 17.—This morning, having been sent a little way out of the city, I took occasion to visit the G———s. They, to whom I was once as father and brother, were all denied to me. I was not suffered to set my foot within the house. Someone hath belied me unto them. Such behaviour is exceeding bitter for flesh to bear, but, thank God, I have a conscience void of offence. Far different was the treatment I received further on at the Wills's. There nothing could be too good for me, though they have less cause to love me than the G——s.

Thur. 18.—Relating to Mr. Robson, of Bristol, the death of Sister Wildash, he told me how a good old man died there of late in like manner, through visiting the condemned prisoners in Newgate. Disregarding the gaol fever, he would gather them about him in one of their dismal cells, sing and pray with them, and read and expound the Scriptures. Some, affected by his kindness, and touched by the hand of God, made confession of their iniquities with bitter tears. He would still pray with them while their irons were being knocked off. Some lost all fear of death, and rejoiced when their turn came. But now the fever hath carried off this good old man who visited them which were sick and in prison, dead in trespasses and sins. Lord, stir me up to act in like manner. A feeling of sluggishness and self-seeking hath, I fear, been again creeping over me.

Sat. 20.—This morning I received a letter from Lady D——, which hath distressed me. I had not suspected Hetty to be of an unsound habit of body, but it seems that from the first her mistress hath feared her too weak for her service, this being all the fault she hath to find in her. She would still fain not part with her, and hath her own physician and apothecary to visit her, besides, says poor Hetty in her little letter which came inside her ladyship's, feeding her up with dainties, and granting her many indulgences. But 'tis plain she fears that she will have to leave, which is a grief to her, it being so good a place.

This news, which gave sorrow to us all, did so to dear Patty likewise, and yet methinks the poor child would fain have her sister home that she might tend her with grateful love, and pour her troubles into her bosom, as she cannot communicate them to her mother because of her sternness, nor to me by reason of my sex.

Sun. 21.—After a revival for a time of the work of God in this place, we have again had a falling away, and 'tis strange the various reasons which men and women, that think themselves of sound mind, give for their leaving us; as some, that we are mere Church of England folk, others that we are mere Dissenters; some, because others whom they love not belong to us; but 'tis fear of man which is the great cause: of parent, husband, wife, brother, sister, kinsman, friend, master, parson, minister, or mob. 'Tis noteworthy that one who said he found he had begun to serve God too soon, and would put off his religion till he was older, meanwhile taking his decent fill of pleasure, was that very night struck down by sickness. Another said she could not find time to come. Can she find time to die? Of those who remain, it were well if some either left likewise, or changed their ways.

If they have not before Mr. Wesley come this way, there will be a weeding with a vengeance to the right hand and the left. Cursers and swearers, drunkards, brawlers, beaters of their wives, and runners after other men's, he will not away with. 'Tis comforting that the little lad, Moody, who was one of the first to find peace with God here, being then scarce eight years of age, hath ever since walked in the light of His countenance.

Mon. 22.—I would not indulge in frivolous jesting, but sometimes, when exasperated by the language of my wife, as to-night touching poor Patty, I have thought that the confusion of tongues was not altogether a curse if it enabled any husband at Babel to turn an ear which did not understand unto the brawling of the partner of his bosom. Mistress Saunders hath been exceeding good to my dear girl, providing her with work at home, and inviting her in private to her house, where she prayed for her as though she had been her own child. Poor Patty no longer scoffs at Methodists and holy things.

I would that my master's growth in grace kept pace with his dear wife's; but I begin to fear that his heart is more bent on laying up treasure upon earth. He seeks reasons to excuse himself from the practice of alms-giving, and, in spite of my faithful service, so far from bestowing on me a share in his business, he hath not even, for a long while, raised my wage.

N.B.—During the singing at church yesterday I noted a curious circumstance. A snake crawled out of its hole under the reading-desk. When the psalm was over it crawled back. Thus at our services hath the devil oft seemed to have given up possession of my heart, but alas! he hath resumed his throne, at the end of our worship.

Tues. 23.—To-day we gathered the grapes upon the gable. Some were pleasant to the taste, and of the rest we are to have a pie. 'Tis possible to find a use for unripe grapes. But what shall be done with him who at the great gathering is found an unripe Christian?

Sun. 28.—'Twas chilling at our meeting to-night to note the smallness of the numbers. Round about the starlings are gathering themselves together for their flight across the sea; but it seems we would rather go solitary on our journey to heaven.

Thurs. Oct. 9.—On this day when, according to our foolish sister, the world should have come to an end, we have held our Public Thanksgiving for our deliverance from the Pretender. O Lord, make us more worthy of Thy mercies. How hast Thou confounded our enemies! When the Prince, as they called him, landed in Scotland —'tis little more than twelve months gone—the wild men flocked about him like bees, and when we were at Newcastle, and the news came that Cope had been routed, and that the Scotch were marching on the town, and then that they were hurrying south on London, men's hearts melted within them like water for terror. But hip and thigh was the enemy smitten at Culloden; and since, their prince hath wandered, like a wolf with a price upon his head. · I had thought that the foolish story of our being on his side had died out, but to-day one threw it at me, adding that 'twas but because the Methodists were cowards and feared to share their punishment, they pretended to rejoice at the discomfiture of the Jacobites.

Fri. 10.—To-day our dear Hetty returned. Now that my eyes are opened, 'tis startling to note the changes which time hath wrought in her. Her mother will have it that she hath been over-worked; but from what she tells us, and I beheld for myself, 'tis plain that this is idle talk. She and Patty met with much contentment, and once more share the same chamber. Her mother can no more twit Patty with burdensomeness. She earns abundant wages, and the dear child offered, if need were, to keep Hetty as well as herself. It grieves me that my wife, by her peevish talk, should put it into our children's heads that we grudge them the shelter of our roof. She means not what she says. Her bark is worse than her bite, for she is not of a cold or a miserly disposition. Why, then, will she let her tongue so wag? I trust that communion with her sister may be of profit to Patty's soul.

Glory to Thy name, O Lord! 'tis plain now that my dear Hetty is Thy child.

Sat. 11.—Within three months three of those who have busied themselves in letting the work of the Lord here, have been summoned to appear suddenly before Him. J—— L—— was drowned in the river; T—— B—— fell from the shaft of his waggon while asleep, the wheel passing over his head; and C—— R——, for very weariness of life and utter misery, blew his brains out, pulling the trigger of his fowling-piece with a string he had fastened to his boot.

Sun. 12.—I could not but call attention to the deaths of these unhappy men in my address this evening, coupling with it the remarkable Providence which we this morning witnessed. Lady D—— coming from the friend's at whose house she tarries, to visit our dear Hetty, as they came down the hill the coach ran upon the horses' haunches, at which they tore down at full gallop, the coach rolling like a ship at sea, and yet never upsetting, nor striking against any of the conveyances going up the hill, between which they ran in and out with nicest care, although the coachman had been thrown to the ground. But a little way beyond the foot of the hill there stood across the road Estridges' cart, full of children, who were going to spend the Sabbath with their grandfather in the country. Before reaching this the horses pulled themselves up dead, as if they had been stopped by an invisible hand (as who shall deny or doubt to have been the case?), and the coachman, who like Lady D—— was unharmed, arriving, drove them as quiet as lambs to our house. Thus doth the Lord watch over them who put their trust in Him. Parson D——, it seems, is of her ladyship's family. Verily the sweet apple and the crab can grow upon one bough.

It gave my dear girl much delight to see her late mistress, and my wife took it as a high honour to have the carriage waiting at the door. Poor Patty would not be seen.

Wed. 15.—At the out-door preaching this evening we had rain all round us, with every now and then a growl of thunder in the distance, but not a drop fell upon the Green until the service was over. Nay, so mild was the air (especially for the season of the year), that Hetty could sit at her open window and hear the whole. 'Tis blessed now, on my return from services, instead of encountering the cold silence of the whole of my family (save for the prattle of my little Susan and Jack), to be able to take sweet counsel with my eldest child. Patty says nothing, but begins to listen with much attention to what passes between us, paying most heed, as is natural, to her sister's words. The Lord make them profitable to her soul.

XX.

Fri. Oct. 17.

 SPENT great part of last night with a poor man who accuses himself of having committed the sin against the Holy Ghost. 'Tis hard to judge whether his bodily sufferings be but the beginning of his punishment for that dreadful sin, or whether, from the effect of these, he labours under delusion. In any case his agonies are awful to behold, and the despair of his set eyes, and to hear the tone, as it were of the tolling of a bell for a funeral without hope for the ungodly, in which he mutters all day long: "All manner of sin and blasphemy shall be forgiven unto men; but the blasphemy against the Holy Ghost shall not be forgiven unto men. And whosoever speaketh a word against the Son of man, it shall be forgiven unto him; but whosoever speaketh against the Holy Ghost, it shall not be forgiven him, neither in this world, neither in the world to come." No

physic takes effect upon him. If misery without hope, and an ever looking forward to worse misery which shall have no end, be hell, then for him hath hell begun on earth.

Thurs. Nov. 6.—Last night we had again a near escape from being burnt in our beds, a narrower than 'twas two year agone, but this time I think not it was malice. None offered to molest my little Jack, and he would fain have tarried longer without, had not the little Susan, who stood at the gate watching for him in her eager care for his safety, told him that Hetty could not sleep for the shouting of the folk; then, though Jack could not stop it, yet would he no longer join in it when he found 'twas burdensome to his sick sister. So the little lad came in, and went to bed when he had taken off his shoes, and crept into Hetty's room to say good-night, and have her kiss.

According to their wont, the foolish folk had left their fires flickering, and the wind, arising in the night, blew up the flames, and drove about the hot embers again fanned alight. We were awoke by a red blaze and a sound of roaring. The house next to ours had caught, and the wind was driving the flames straight down upon us. I bade my family secure such few things as they could lay their hands on, and having wrapped poor Hetty in blankets, was about to bear her to a friend's, when suddenly the wind shifted and drave back the flames, and then lulling, the fire was got under, though not until such damage had been done to our neighbour's house that 'twas necessary to spread his family for lodging throughout the village. O Lord, how can we render unto Thee thanks sufficient for Thy goodness in so manifestly putting forth Thy hand to save ourselves?

Fri. 7.—To-night we saw the Northern Lights. Yea, the curtains being drawn back, at times I still see their strangely wavering brightness, methinks like no other light I wot of. 'Twas between eight and nine they began to play, and many thought the Day of Judgment had begun, that the Son of man had indeed come like a thief in the night. And 'tis not wonderful. Their light is passing strange, now as of heaven opening, and anon as the reflection of a world on fire. I went up into Hetty's chamber. She looked calmly upon the sky; but Patty, on her knees, had buried her face in the bedclothes. O Lord, Thou wilt not quench the smoking flax, nor break the bruised reed!

Sat. 8.—'Tis strange, I thought the devil had been chained, but I was wrong. To-night, as I walked in the fields like Isaac, preparing my mind for the Sabbath by meditation, and thinking over what I should say upon the morrow,—suddenly, although no man was nigh ('twas dusk, but not dark, and I was in an open part of the field, far from bush or tree), suddenly I was struck to the ground, as though by the stroke of a cudgel. And when I rose, I was again struck down, and so again a third time. But after that I was no more molested save that when I rose the third time, a savage voice, as of one thwarted, growled in my ears, "Go thy ways then."

In the next field I met poor Daniel Reed, who hath so often been almost persuaded to become a Christian, but the drink hath proved too strong for him. He had then had more than was good for either body or soul; but would not be persuaded from going on into the village to get more. He hath solemnly promised me, nevertheless, that he will keep sober to-morrow, and come to the preaching in the evening. Was it to prevent this the Evil One put forth his power to buffet me?

Sun. 9.—Poor Daniel was not at the meeting. I doubt not he gave me his word in good faith, but who can believe a man given to strong drink? His will is not his own.

Mon. 10, MORNING.—Before I go in to business, I must record a marvellous experience. About midnight I was awoke by a strange scrambling and scratching outside our front house wall. I opened the window, but could see nothing. The moon was shining clear, and all was still, but as soon as I drew in my head, I heard the sound again, and my wife awaking heard it likewise, and with as much dismay. 'Twas as though a man with heavy boots would clamber up the wall, and one with great iron claws prevented him. Jack's little dog moreover, which lay on the mat outside his chamber door, was awakened by the noise; but, instead of barking according to his wont, crept under our bed where he shook and sweat exceedingly. What may this portend?

EVENING.—Daniel Reed hath been found drowned hard by the Ferry. Drunken companions persuaded him to break his promise to me yesterday, and with them he went Sabbath-breaking beyond the river. After nightfall he suddenly started up from the drink, swearing that though the devil had kept him from the preaching, he would speak with the preacher, after all, that night, as he had passed his word. Verily, Satan is loosed for a season, and is going about in our midst, seeking whom he may devour.

Wed. 12.—We have had a weary time of dread. Last evening little Jack went into the wood, and wandered in it till he lost his way. Our neighbours joined us in our search, but 'twas not until long after noon to-day we found him, asleep upon a heap of dead leaves, being worn out by his wanderings. Although the wood is large, 'tis strange he heard not our shouts; and stranger, he says that Daniel Reed came out of the brushwood and beckoned to him; but that, being afraid, he ran away. Until her brother was brought back the little Susan was beside herself. O Lord, I thank Thee for Thy goodness in preserving and restoring unto me my dear boy.

Thurs. 13.—Verily Mammon hath entered into the heart of my master. He chid me for being absent from my place yesterday, saying that there were enow to search for the boy without me. Without his own father! Methinks, Mr. Saunders of late hath not treated me with due respect, being puffed up by his increasing substance, and forgetting that 'tis to my industry and integrity the increase, under Providence, is largely owing. Other traders know this, and, peradventure, Mr. Saunders may discover it to his cost, if he give any hint of a wish to be rid of me.

Mon. 24.—I have not been honoured to receive a letter from him I reverence next to God and my Saviour, Mr. Wesley, since I writ my mind to him so freely (albeit, I still think with due respect); but he hath sent Mistress Saunders an account of news he hath received from our brethren in Flanders, one, my dear friend Staniforth. The armies have lain so near that our sentries and the French have taken snuff with one another. Truly I think this better than gunpowder. But there hath been sharp fighting, so that our men were forced to flee. Of the brethren one is dead, and another left upon the field. Would that the reign of the Prince of Peace had begun! The brethren went into action exhorting their unconverted comrades to seek the forgiveness of their sins, so that they might have like confidence with themselves in the presence of death.

Tues. 25.—Some of the brethren who left us have formed themselves into a new society. A strange society for them who would be called saints! Save that it meets not at a tavern, but at the house of one of the members, wherein it differs from a gathering of worldly men 'twere hard to tell. True, the Bible is put upon the table, but it is never opened, 'tis said, until it be nigh time to break up, and in like manner prayer is huddled off to the fag end of the meeting, when a few words must suffice. The time is spent in drinking (I say not to excess, but in a manner unbecoming them which name the name of Christ, more particularly on the night of the Sabbath), and in talking over the affairs of the nation and the neighbourhood. The Vicar, the churchwardens, and overseers are much ridiculed and abused, and doubtless their words and deeds are oft foolish and worthy of censure. ('Tis no later than last week that the parson's man, doubtless sent by his master, came to my house to make inquiry whether I "had a-got better o' my complaint," meaning my religion.) Nevertheless, methinks, 'tis not seemly for men that have learnt their catechism, instead of ordering themselves lowly and reverently to all their betters, thus to assemble to speak evil of their governors, teachers, spiritual pastors and masters.

Wed. 26 (Nay, 'tis Thurs. Morning).—Again the blessed Spirit is at work. As I went to Bath in the morning, I heard one say to another with a laugh, that Roger Cawson had gone mad. I knew what that meant. In the first days the workings of the Spirit were put down to drunkenness, and now when a man seeks Christ, 'tis said he is gone crazy. That worldly men should so judge, perchance is not to be wondered at, for 'twas with a distraught air Roger walked into my house to-night, without his hat, although snow had begun to fall. He came up to me, but said nothing; turned upon his heel, and fled. Again he came, but my family being in the room, again he held his peace. I chanced to be alone when he came the third time, and putting down his mouth to my ear, he asked me in horror how he should escape hell-fire. Thinking I should have a better opportunity of speaking to him there, I persuaded him to return home, and accompanied him thither; he clinging to my arm, trembling and groaning all the way. I found his wife and children in little better case, nay, not so good; all weeping, not for their sins, but for fear the head of the family had gone out of his wits and they should come to want. Finding that they had no ear for spiritual consolations, I persuaded them to go to bed, promising that I would remain with Roger. Then down we dropt upon our knees, and for some hours I wrestled with God in prayer on his behalf. 'Twas not until I had exhorted him to cease crying simply to be saved from hell-fire, to acknowledge himself a vile sinner, and humble himself in the dust, whatever should be the Almighty's will concerning him, that the Lord spake peace to his soul.

"Glory be to God!" he exclaimed. "I was down at the bottom of a coal-pit, and now heaven's opened, and I can see the angels through the floor,—a sinner saved by grace. Thanks be unto the Lord Jesus Christ."

His wife, who had crept down, stood wondering. I encouraged her to seek the same blessed Saviour; but alas! she seemed to derive more comfort from my assurance that her husband would doubtless return, and with renewed energy, to his worldly calling in the morning.

Sat. Dec. 13.—The work having so increased that 'tis impossible to find room for them which come in any private house, and the hard weather forbidding our meeting in the open air, I have made bold to ask for the use of the granary at the old Maltings, which now stand idle. Methinks that one or other of our farmers might have found room for us, but they professed themselves unable. God grant I be not guilty of lack of charity, but methinks they had spoken more truly had they said unwilling. . The manager for the Maltings Trustees showed me more courtesy, at once granting my request; and 'tis expected that to-morrow evening a great multitude will assemble in the granary. The Lord grant that my words may be blessed to their souls. I thank Thee for Thy goodness in again lifting up the light of Thy countenance upon me. Old times have come back. I, that have been despised, am once more called honourable.

Sun. 14, MIDNIGHT.—Although I was bruised in the catastrophe, and ache in every limb with running from sufferer to sufferer, I know 'twould be vain to retire to rest. For the present sleep hath forsook mine eyes, though weariness weigheth down my eyelids. Before recording the occurrences of this awful night, I would again offer up to Thee, O God, my humble and heartfelt thanks for Thy goodness in once more suffering me to be the living to praise Thee. O Lord, be merciful unto the afflicted, and pour the oil and wine of Thy consolations into the hearts of the bereaved. Grant that they may be able to say, " The Lord gave, and the Lord hath taken away. Blessed be the name of the Lord."

When I awoke in the morning I was filled with strange misgivings as to the evening preaching. But these forebodings I set aside, partly because I thought 'twould be cowardly self-seeking, a weak yielding to the flesh, did I, as I had more than once been minded to do, give up the preaching, since, in the course of the day, I had heard that the sons of Belial had banded themselves to muster at it for tumult. But partly, I fear, 'twas through vainglory. I would not lose mine opportunity of speaking to so large a congregation, amongst them, doubtless, false brethren who had belittled me.

A great multitude gathered in the granary in the evening, and all went well until I had given out my text, "Prepare to meet thy God," when lo! with no warning, but a sudden creak and crack, the floor gave way, and the lights being extinguished, the whole congregation fell through into the warehouses and stables beneath.

'Twas terrible to hear the screams of pain and shrieks for help in the horror of deep darkness, and when lights were brought, owing to the clouds of dust, there was at first but little to be seen. I fell upon the top, and beyond a few slight bruises and scratches, without which scarce any escaped, had, thanks to the protecting hand of the Lord, received no harm.

With others in like case, and those who had rushed up at the sound of the crash, I set to work to save the sufferers, who were writhing and tossing in a heap of heads and bodies, legs and arms, hands, feet, boards, beams, as it might have been in a foundering ship.

Considering the numbers, 'tis marvellous there were so few injuries of moment; nevertheless, bones have been broken, and alas! there are three dead, two strangers, and one of this village, Roger Cawson. Thank God, he had found peace.

The strangers have taken away their dead and wounded in carts. They talk angrily, as if they had been lured hither to their destruction.

Fri. 19.—Save that many will be laid aside for a long while, the sufferers in this parish are doing well, but two more of the strangers have died of their wounds. I fear that this great gathering, to which I had looked forward as a means of bringing many to the Lord, may for a time stop the good work in this place. If this be in any degree through my unfaithfulness, I humble myself in the dust before God. Nevertheless, my blood must boil at the charges which men bring against me. As though I had not enough soreness of heart, some talk as if I should be hanged for reckless risking of folk's lives, while others openly hint 'twas worse. God grant that they who so shamefully assail my character be not themselves answerable for a devilish deed wrought to bring discredit on our cause, since more of the vulgar say 'tis manifest from this that God is set against us. Poor Cawson's wife now uses bitter words against me, and anon weeps bitterly at the thought that her man should ever have been murdered, as she saith, through having been fool enough to listen to me and turn Methodist.

Sun. 21.—This afternoon I went to poor Roger Cawson's funeral. But why call I him poor? He is safe with Christ in God. There was a great gathering at the burial, and most looked upon me with unfriendly, if not downright angry eyes. I was not at church in the morning, but I am told that in his sermon the Vicar declared openly that the fall of the granary floor was a judgment from God upon the Methodists.

And yet how oft hath he read with his lips, and heard with his ears, although he hath not listened or comprehended with his understanding, "Suppose ye that these Galileans were sinners above all the Galileans, because they suffered such things? Or those eighteen upon whom the tower in Siloam fell, and slew them, think ye that they were sinners above all men that dwelt in Jerusalem? I tell you, Nay; but except ye repent, ye shall all likewise perish."

So said He who spake as never man spake. Would that they would take to heart His solemn words, "Except ye repent, ye shall all likewise perish." The Vicar, moreover, 'tis said, affirmed that the Trustees of the Maltings, being churchmen, ought to hide their heads for lending their ward's property to Methodists, and should be brought to account in Chancery for the damage done unto the same. Though they know not the Gospel, our beneficed clergy know something of the law in matters of property. Still this seems to me fond talk. Nevertheless the manager hath taken affright at it, unjustly accusing me of coming whining to him, and cursing, with much profane language, the hour in which he listened to me. Why could I not have gone to some fellow of my own kidney, some other sneak? he asked. Verily, the Lord hath humbled me, if, as I fear, 'tis true, I was unduly puffed up by believing that God was again working by my hands, and seeing myself once more held in honour here. "Pride goeth before destruction, and a haughty spirit before a fall."

Notwithstanding my assiduous attendance on the sufferers, were anything to happen to them in the present temper of the people, methinks I should have to flee for my life, if suffered to escape with it.

Wed. 24.—My little Jack, who of late had grown well liked in the village, came in complaining of having been stoned; grieved not at the hurt, but the indignity. I would that they which be angry against me would have the manliness to visit their wrath upon myself, and leave my innocent boy alone.

Thurs. 25.—With sufferers and glooming faces around us this hath been a dull Christmas. Our dear Hetty, moreover, hath, alas! begun to spit blood. But, Lord, I thank Thee for Thy goodness in answering my prayer. Once more I have the whole of my family under my roof, and on the heart of my poor Patty likewise Thy gracious Spirit hath begun its work. Glory for ever to Thy Name!

Wed. 31.—Another year is drawing to a close. Its sands are nigh run out. As numerous, as innumerable have been Thy mercies, O my heavenly Father. Some experiences I have had to humble and to sadden, but these, too, I count among my mercies, for if we bear not the cross, how can we expect to wear the crown?

We held our little watch-night at home, but for dear Hetty's sake, who would fain sit up with us to the last, waited not for midnight before we ceased. My beloved Patty is now an open seeker after salvation. Is not that by itself enough to make my heart run over with thanksgiving? Alas! that so sweet a child should ever have been tempted by a worthless villain into sin; but if this be the fruit of her fall, I no longer repine at Thy mysterious Providence, O my Father.

XXI.

1747—Jan. 23.

ALAS, alas! But what words can express my anguish? News came to us in Bath that Mr. Wesley was yesterday thrown from his horse and killed. Oh that we had parted last in the fulness of our first friendship! That great, good, noble man! My younger in years, but my father in Christ. O Lord, Thy providences are indeed mysterious! Who shall supply his loss? Never before have I seen my master so moved. Although in the thick of business, which hath again set in strongly after the dead season of the holidays, he at once followed his wife's counsel and took horse for Bristol. Mistress Saunders hath it strongly borne in upon her that the report, although we received it with many particular circumstances, is false, the invention of an enemy. If it be not a lie, she says, Bristol will witness such a funeral as hath not been seen in memory of man; but still she cheerfully returns to her belief that *'tis* a lie. God grant her words prove true.

Sat. 24.—Glory be to God! Mr. Saunders came back last night with glad tidings. 'Twas not a malicious report, but only exaggerated. The following is a true account of what happened. On Thursday, Mr. Wesley, having to preach at Wick, mounted shortly after dinner. While riding through St. Nicholas Gate, he saw a cart that had turned sharp from Nicholas Street coming fast down hill. There was space, and no more, between the wall for Mr. Wesley to have gone by, had not the driver, although shouted to, being either deaf or pig-headed, blocked the way. Unwilling to ride him down, Mr. Wesley, risking a life of so much greater worth, pulled back his horse. The shaft struck the poor beast on the shoulder and knocked him down, Mr. Wesley flying over his ears like a stone from a sling, and falling in the mud between the wheel and the wall. The cart went by without harming him. A little dirt, which was soon wiped off in a neighbouring shop, at first appeared all the hurt that he had gotten. Mounting again, he reached Wick at the appointed time, and returned to Bristol in time to preach on "Thou, Lord, shalt save both man and beast." Afterward, he found that he was somewhat bruised, but application of warm treacle dulled the pain within an hour. Thus doth the Lord watch over His saints.

N.B.—Treacle is indeed a sovereign salve. 'Tis no wonder Mr. Wesley wearies not of advising it. I have proved its virtues on my Jacky, who is ever bruising himself.

Mon. 26.—Mr. Wesley hath again visited us, and, I thank the Lord, I am restored to a measure of his favour. After speaking with my accusers, he came back, and holding out his hand, said frankly, " Brother, I believe I have done you wrong in my judgment of you." Still 'tis not as it was before. 'Tis with friendship as with crockery, which, when broken, may be mended, but the crack remains. His visit was a great comfort to Hetty and Patty. My poor dear girls drank in his words as if spoken by more than mortal man. I rejoiced at their consolation, and yet, so weak is human nature, I grudged the coming in of any mere man, however great and good, between myself and my children. They are my children, not only according to the flesh, but in the Lord. O God, forgive me for my wicked, my unthankful spirit of jealousy.

My business calling me to the Devizes next Thursday, I shall once more see and hear the beloved man. He purposes to preach there then, being encouraged by the mastery which the Lord gave him over the mob the week before last.

When he rode in, he says, the town was in a tumult,

as if the French had entered; one who should have known better stirring up the baser sort, and encouraging them in their vile language, having first posted on the walls and displayed in the shop windows more obsceneness of his own. But "the grace of our Lord Jesus Christ" ('twas those few words, as full of meaning as an egg of meat, Mr. Wesley took for his text) was too strong for the mob and its master. They would fain have barked, but were constrained to hold their tongues. God grant they continue not mere dumb dogs, but be converted into true Christians, eager to utter their praises of God for what He hath done for their souls.

Sat. 31.—'Twas very quiet at the Devizes on Thursday. The mob mutinied against its master, and held its peace. A few boys, who will be for ever shouting, whatever the cause, or for no cause at all, and a drunken soldier or two of a different stamp from our pious dragoons, were all that he could muster, although 'twas market day. (*N.B.*—Mr. Bramham's money was a shilling short.) A cloth-buyer in the public room of the inn at which I lay declared openly before his fellows that he had been at the preaching, and had never heard a better sermon in his life; and when they jeered him, saying 'twas the first he ever heard, and challenged him to give the text, he gave it with great solemnity: "All have sinned and come short of the glory of God;" and gave them likewise good part of the sermon, so that they soon ceased their funning. Yesterday morning the text was, "He healeth them that are broken in heart." 'Tis wondrous the different ways Mr. Wesley hath to move. The day before he had roughly drawn the harrows over men's hearts, but now he gently dropped on them the dew. When he set forth for London, not a tongue wagged against him; nay, many uncovered as he rode by.

My affairs holding me in the town, I came upon many unlikely spots in which, as in the case of the cloth-buyer, the seed sown had already begun to spring up.

To my sorrow, I learnt likewise that my master makes bargains which pass not through my books. I like not this wool and horse business. For the wool I would say nothing, if above board, but what doth my master know of horses? Nevertheless, one spoke confidently of meeting him at the Horse Fair next month. He can but make himself a laughing-stock. And were he competent to the business, 'tis not one, methinks, in which a Christian man should engage. The horse hath rightly been called a noble animal; therefore, 'tis strange that to the buying and selling of him there go more lies and cheating than pass in bargains over any other kind of bestial.

Sat. Feb. 14.—The weather hath of late been very mild, to the comfort of poor Hetty, whom, in spite of all our fires, the cold had pinched. 'Tis sweet to see the care dear Patty hath of her, screening her from every draught as if a green-house plant, and in the midst of all the work for pay which, in spite of my remonstrances (therein alone resisting my authority), she will persist in doing, finding time to make her sister wraps and scarfs of woollen. But she is always ready to do anything for all. Verily I think that, in Patty, Mary and Martha have met. I cannot doubt that she hath not only chosen, but gained, that good part which shall not be taken away from her; although this she will not claim to have secured, being unable to point to any exact time in which the Lord first spoke peace to her soul.

So very mild was the weather to-day that dear Hetty could sit at the open window. Being at home, going through the books of a customer of my master's, who hath become bankrupt (poor man, he is no knave, though inspection of his accounts is all the security he hath to offer), I could overhear my dear children's converse. There was now no idle talk of valentines as aforetime, although the pairing birds were twittering on the trees. Primroses are out, and of these and snowdrops Susan and Jack make posies for their sick sister. Notwithstanding the mildness of the weather, she hath a foreboding that she will never be abroad again until carried to the churchyard, and loves to have the flowers brought to her, as she cannot go to them. Thanks be unto the Lord, she hath now no fear of death, speaking of her approaching end with more calmness than we can bear to listen to. After such talk I have found my poor Patty in an agony of weeping.

Mon. 16.—What a change in a few hours. The snow lies deep upon the ground, and a cutting north wind hath been blowing all day, finding its way into the house, in spite of all our care to keep it out; and bringing back worse than ever our poor Hetty's hacking cough. But she bears her sufferings with Christian patience, and thinks not of herself, but others. She could find time to ask whether the wild birds had been fed—Susan and Jack had before made them their care, shovelling and sweeping the snow from the backyard, and scattering crumbs. 'Tis strange to note their tameness; larks, thrushes, and blackbirds, coming to the very door, and scarce taking more pains than pigeons to avoid being trodden under foot.

Wed. 18.—With difficulty I made my way to and from the city; many of the roads, 'tis said, are quite impassable, filled to the very top of the walls and hedges. I hear of folk snowed up, and of travellers and carriers overwhelmed in the snow, and of coaches that have been with difficulty dug out. The frost has nipped the evergreens brown and black, as if they had been singed and burnt with fire. Notwithstanding all our care to warm the bed-chambers, the water froze last night in the ewers into solid lumps. 'Twas pitiful to-day to see the little birds lying dead upon the road. Rabbits and hares have invaded our garden, but I fear the poor starving half-stupid creatures get little for their pains in digging. "He giveth snow like wool: He scattereth the hoar-frost like ashes. He casteth forth His ice like morsels; who can stand against His cold?"

Wed. 25.—The weather is milder again, which is a relief to our poor sufferer, and to us on her account. Joan and Frances, who are as inseparable as Susan and Jack, brought home violets and daffodils from their walk to-day. The violets fill Hetty's chamber with their odour. At the sight of them, the first this year, the dear child's eyes brightened as I have not seen them since the winter set in.

Fri. 27.—To-day I met poor Robert A——, but he passed me hastily without speaking, whether from shame or hatred I cannot say. Alas! how is the very fashion of his countenance altered since his fall from grace. 'Tis plain he hath no peace, and who can wonder? And 'tis said that his trade, for the bettering of which he left us, is fast falling off. O Lord, restore unto him health, peace, the joy of Thy salvation. Heal his backsliding, O Thou who hast said, "I will love them freely, for mine anger is turned away."

It cut me to the heart to see one whose face once shone with the oil of holy gladness, and whose gait in his eagerness to do good was as the bounding of a roe, creeping along with that dreary downcast look.

Sat. 28.—I have received this letter from poor Robert:—

"FRIEND PIDGEON,—The sight of you to-day brought back to me the memory of the blessedness I have enjoyed in days gone by, when we took sweet counsel together. My present lot is misery, and I can see no hope, for I have crucified the Lord afresh, and spoken falsely of His servants. You in particular have no cause to love me, for I confess, with shame, I have told of you abominable lies. But, oh, take pity on my wretchedness. I can find no rest for the sole of my foot, and have no ark to go back to. I am like the unclean spirit walking through dry places. Oh, tell me if you think that yet there may be hope, that I can repent with acceptable repentance. Forgive my base conduct towards you, and answer me whether you believe that God can forgive so black a sinner. I am nigh beside myself with present anguish, and fearful looking forward to the judgment to come."

Sat. March 7.—Yesterday I attended Shepton Mallet

market, to meet farmers with whom my master hath dealings (he is open now as to his wool trade, nor can I see why, save to transact business in which I had no hand, he should ever have concealed it), and likewise to call upon the clothworkers and stockingers.

'Tis a town much set against Methodism, as I had heard from Mr. Wesley, and learnt more fully from Brother Stone, whose acquaintance I made.

The last time Mr. Wesley was at Shepton, a drunken mob had been gathered by tuck of drum to assault him, but not alighting, according to his wont, at Brother Stone's, he was enabled to preach in peace. Having found that they had waited in vain, the mob came back and pelted Mr. Wesley from the preaching place to Brother Stone's, afterwards battering the door and breaking the windows. One of the mob, a ringleader, chancing to be shut in the house when the rush was made, was struck on the head; whereupon he, piteously, being in fear of death, entreated Mr. Wesley to tell him what he must do; and having been bidden to pray, fell upon his knees, and began to pray with might and main. Having prayed himself, Mr. Wesley, went down, and walked out of the back door as the mob broke in at the front, and finally escaped unharmed; the mob, in their anger at having been deprived of their prey, being with difficulty restrained from burning down the house. On another occasion, drunken men, at the prompting of the Curate, of like kidney with our Vicar, howled a psalm to throw out the Methodists, but their singing was too strong for them. Afterward the ringleader shouted a mock sermon, his congregation meantime pelting those of the brethren who, owing to the throng, were forced to stand at the doors of the preaching place. Mr. Wesley would fain have gone out to the rioters, and doubtless would have quelled them, had not the brethren taken him off his legs, and held him back by force until the mob dispersed.

April 19. EASTER DAY.—'Tis sad that now the fine weather hath come, dear Hetty cannot get out of doors to taste it. This day hath been most lovely. Our cherry trees and plum trees are as white with blossom as in winter with snow, and the apple trees are coming out. The girls yesterday brought their sister from the wood a handful of wild strawberry blossom, and to-day we heard the cuckoo for the first time. All day long the doves have been cooing in the woods, and our pigeons on the roof. It hath been a day of sunshine and of peace, but our poor sufferer hath been compelled to keep her chamber. Besides the cough, her strength fast fails her, and she hath cold sweats. Thanks be unto Thee, O Lord, her heart is fixed, her soul is stayed on Thee. Patty hath not left her all day, and, doubtless. it being a work both of necessity and mercy, hath derived as much profit from their communion in the sick chamber as though she had assembled herself with the public congregation. She hath been reading to her sister of the resurrection in the Gospels. 'Tis a history in which dear Hetty takes exceeding delight, not alone for the assurance it gives unto her own hopes of heaven, but as recording the triumph of her beloved Lord and Saviour after His sufferings and death. Such love as women bear to the blessed Jesus is seldom found, methinks, in the colder hearts of men.

Mon. 20.—To-day at an old book shop in the High Street, I picked up, for a shilling and a few pence, a strange old Bible. Methought that it might give pleasure to dear Hetty, but 'tis the teaching of the Bible, not the curious guises of form and print in which it may be found, wherein she takes delight, and she careth not to hear the promises which are her comfort in any other than the exact words to which she hath been accustomed. I shall, therefore, to-morrow despatch it in a parcel to Mr. Wesley. I know little of such matters, but methinks that they who be judges would value it at far higher price than that I gave for it this morning, notwithstanding that it hath but one cover, and no title-page. The spelling is exceeding quaint. To the New Testament there is a title-page, with representations of the Twelve

Tribes and the Twelve Apostles. Thereon and at the end is this inscription, "Imprinted at London by the Deputies of Christopher Barker, Printer to the Queenes most Excellent Maiestie, 1599." Both Old Testament and New are furnished with summaries, expositions, and annotations, in small type on the margins, and likewise with maps and pictures exceeding quaint. The latter part of the seventh verse of the third chapter of Genesis is thus Englished, "And they sewed figge-tree leaves together and made themselves breeches." There is bound up with the Bible a Psalter with the music at the head of every psalm, the semibreves and minims being of a diamond shape. By way of preface to the whole is given the following :—

"Of the incomparable treasure of the holy Scriptures, with a prayer for the true use of the same.

Esai. 12. 8 & 49. 10.	Here is the spring where waters flowe,
Rom. 21. 16 & 22. 17.	to quench our heate of sinne :
	Here is the tree where trueth doth growe
Jerem. 33. 15.	to leade our lives therein.
Psal. 119. 160.	Here is the judge that stints the strife,
Rev. 2. 7 & 22. 2.	when men's devices faile ;
Psal. 119. 142, 144.	Here is the bread that feedes the life,
John 6. 35.	that death cannot assaile.
	The tidings of salvation deare,
Luke 2. 10.	Comes to our ears from hence :
	The fortresse of our faith is here,
Ephes. 6. 16.	and shielde of our defence.

T

	Then be not like the hogge that hath
Matth. 7. 6.	a pearle at his desire,
	And takes more pleasure in the trough,
2 Pet. 2. 32.	and wallowing in the mire.
	Reade not this book in any case,
Matth. 6. 22.	but with a single eye:
	Reade not but first desire God's grace,
Psal. 119. 27, 73.	to understand thereby.
	Pray still in faith with this respect
Jude 20.	to fructifie therein,
	That knowledge may bring this effect
Psal. 119. 11.	to mortifie thy sinne.
	Then happy thou in all thy life,
Joshua 1. 8.	whatso to thee befalles.
Pasl. 1. 1, 2.	Yea, double happie shalt thou be,
Psal. 94. 12, 13.	when God by death thee calles.

"O Gratious God, and most merciful Father, which hast vouchsafed us the rich and precious jewell of thy holy word, assist us with thy Spirit, that it may be written in our hearts to our everlasting comfort, to reform us, to renew us according to thine owne image, to build us up, and edifie us unto the perfect building of thy Christ, sanctifying and increasing in us all heavenly vertues. Graunt this, O heavenly Father, for Jesus Christes sake. Amen."

The book bears many names, and would seem to have been diligently perused. Would that men did thus now read their Bibles.

Sat. June 20.—I am again to have the privilege of journeying with Mr. Wesley. My master's brother at

St. Ives having persuaded him to engage in the pilchard-curing (I pray he have not too many irons in the fire), I am to proceed thither on business of the coming season, and Mr. Wesley, journeying at this time down to Cornwall, hath given permission for me to ride with him.

XXII.

Perranwell.—*Mon. June* 29.

HITHERTO hath the Lord helped us. At Plymouth Dock on Friday, a great crowd had assembled, bent on mischief, but Mr. Wesley lighting from his horse, and speaking with the fiercest of them, suddenly there was, for a time, a great calm, but when we had gotten inside the house, they bombarded it with their bricks and stones until their strength failed them. Through all God watched over us. Not a hair of our heads was hurt. Next day when Mr. Wesley had gone out to preach in the street, came an officer with soldiers and drums, a fierce mob following, their ringleader towering over them by the head and shoulders like Saul. But Mr. Wesley having taken him by the hand, he swore that he would knock down any who molested us, and opened a way for us to our lodgings, the crowd opening before him like the sea before a ship.

St. Ives, *Tues.* 30.—We arrived in time to go to morning prayers. The church is hard by the sea. We heard the waves beating against the churchyard wall. 'Tis said that in times past the sea hath washed over the church itself. Within, amongst other quaint devices, is carved a blacksmith, with the furniture of his forge, the likeness of him who made the ironwork of the church.

There is no clamour here against the Methodists, but the town is all agog concerning the coming election for Parliament men. No business can be done till that be over.

Thurs. July 2—The election is ended, and the day hath passed without riot. At the preaching and the Society meeting this evening, the lukewarm were stirred up to greater earnestness, and backsliders cried for mercy. 'Tis said that through the election no Methodist hath taken a bribe. Nay, none hath entered the houses thrown open with abundance of free meat and drink to win men's votes.

Tues. 7.—Mr. Wesley hath returned to St. Ives. On Saturday, as my business will have been accomplished, in less time than had been allowed me, I shall join him at St. Just, and travel with him back to Bristol.

St. Just, *Sat.* 11.—At Gulval, where he preached yesterday, Mr. Wesley tells me there is a spring hard by the church they call the Gulf Well, of which ignorant and superstitious folk credit the following :—

If it be asked whether such an one be alive, in sound health, sick, or dead; if alive, clear water will bubble up; if sick, muddy water; if dead, there is no stirring of the waters.

PENZANCE, *Sun.* 12.—Methinks Mr. Wesley must have lungs of leather and a frame of brass. This morning he preached at five at St. Just; at noon, to a great multitude at Morvah, which 'tis said, signifieth "the place by the sea," though in this part of England 'twould be hard to find a place far from it. We attended service in Zennor Church, in a wild rocky country hard by the Gurnard's Head, where many a stout ship hath been cast away. After prayers, Mr. Wesley preached under the churchyard wall. And after that at Newlyn by Penzance, where thousands had gathered themselves together. For a time there was confusion, drunken men who had come over from Penzance rushing and hustling in the throng, so that some were thrown down, and Mr. Wesley hurried from the sandbank on which he stood, into the midst of them which crowded together on the slope. But this aroused the wrath of a Newlyn man, who, though before much set against the Methodists, swore that none, at peril of his life, should molest the preacher; and after that, there was peace. Thus doth God raise us up champions from among our enemies.

TERDINNY, *Tues.* 14.—To-morrow I must set out for

Bath, my master having sent orders to that end to St. Ives, whence Mr. James Saunders hath sent them on by a mounted man. 'Tis a cross not to be permitted to continue to accompany Mr. Wesley in his journeying in this country, for our hearts are again knit together in love; but I must obey. Yesterday Mr. Wesley preached here to a great congregation, who listened earnestly, notwithstanding the slanders against him which the clergyman of this parish (St. Buryan's) hath spread abroad, yea, proclaimed from the pulpit. Amongst other things, it seems, he declared that Mr. W. had sent down a letter, requiring the poor people here to raise and at once send him one hundred pounds. Mr. Wesley hath writ to the Rector, requiring him to withdraw this lying charge as openly as it was made.

'Tis said there is but one church tower higher in the county than St. Buryan's. From it may be seen the Scilly Isles. In the churchyard there is an ancient cross carved with a representation of the Saviour and His wounds, and another without the yard.

Tues. 21.—When I left home, dear Hetty for a time had somewhat rallied, and though I could not but fear that the hope was fond, nevertheless I flattered myself with the thought that, peradventure, the Lord might yet spare her to us. But on my return home I found the dear child worse than I have before seen her. The excessive heat of the last few days hath so prostrated her that her languid life hath become a burden unto her. She hath but one desire, to depart and be with Christ. Although that be far better for the dear child, 'twill be with a heart full of sad foreboding I shall again journey into Cornwall next month. 'Tis hard to give up our children even to the Almighty, and to find that they have begun to sit loose to earthly love. Methinks that 'tis to Patty alone her heart now clings, although she ever strives to treat her mother and myself with affection and respect, and to express her gratitude to Joan and Frances for the thoughtfulness with which the children strive to humour what they believe to be her likings (though of these she hath now but few); and she hath ever a smile, which, though loving, is very mournful to behold, for the little Susan and Jacky. 'Tis strange to see how Jacky who in her health treated his eldest sister lovingly indeed, but with no great deference, now looks upon her with a kind of awe. The little Susan steals about the room as silent as a shadow or a sunbeam, and in her wish to show her love, but anxiety to give no trouble, kisses her sister's shawl behind her back.

Thurs. 23.—Lady D——, who is again tarrying with her friend, drove to the house to-day, bringing with her a basket of apricots for Hetty. The poor child was cheered by the visit of her mistress, but cared not for the fruit. 'Tis so little she eats with relish, we had hoped that it might tempt her. But she seemed to take more pleasure in a sheaf of white lilies the children brought her from the garden, and prayed that the apricots might be shared among them. Never before have I seen lilies so fine and so plenty as they are this year.

ST. IVES, *Tues. Aug.* 4.—They were cutting the oats and barley as I rode hither. The crops look well, and there seems fair prospect of good weather, but here 'tis of another harvest they think. May the Lord of harvests bless both the husbandmen, and the ploughers and reapers and gleaners of the sea.

Wed. 5.—Some place, whose name hath escaped me, was built, they say, in a parable, on herring-bones. Here 'twould be pilchards. During my former visit to the town there was much talk of the fish, but now there is scarce aught else in the minds and mouths of men, women, or children. Watchers are posted on the hills with boughs to wave signal to the boats in waiting of the coming of the shoals. Schools they call them. 'Tis said they turn the water red.

Sat. 8.—This morning, before breakfast, the news ran through the town that the pilchards had come, and all the inhabitants poured out, like swarming bees from their hive, to behold and rejoice.

Mon. 17.—There have been great catches, and nigh

every one on shore is busy in the salting. Methinks my master must be satisfied with the reports I take him home next week, if things so continue. One net hath broke, which gave me occasion to speak last night on the miraculous Draught of Fishes. Methinks, if preachers more frequently made it their business to study the callings with particulars of which they illustrate their discourses, they would make their sermons more acceptable to them that be conversant with the same, who now, noting and deriding their ignorance of worldly matters, are too apt to hold their spiritual teaching likewise in contempt. The sights which I have witnessed here enabled me to speak with understanding of the inclosing of a great multitude of fishes, and the beckoning " unto their partners, which were in the other ship that they should come and help them." Here, without miracle, hundreds of thousands of fish are sometimes enclosed in the great nets. 'Tis a sight never to be forgotten when the tuck has gone round the seine, and the fish are hauled up, and scooped out, flashing like silver, in baskets, to be emptied into the boats gathered around.

Wed. 19.—The Mayor having honoured me by bidding me with Mr. Saunders, in spite of my Methodism, which I trust I have taken no pains to cloak, I have dined to-day with the Corporation. Poor Sarah would be proud, and think that at length I stood on the road to advancement; but though I would not speak with disrespect of my host, who treated me with great hospitality, disregarding the lowliness of my condition (that is, if a report, most unfounded, have not got abroad that I am partner in the business of the Brothers Saunders), I feel that it would not be for the good of my soul to share oft in such festivities. A loving-cup of silver-gilt went round, with an inscription which I made bold to ask his Worship's leave to copy :—

> "If any discord 'twixt my friends arise
> Within the borough of beloved St. Ives,
> It is desyred that this, my cup of love,
> To every one a peacemaker may prove ;
> Then I am blest to have given a legacie
> So like my harte unto posteritie.
> —FRANCIS BASSETT, 1640."

This gentleman, the giver of the cup, was then member for the borough. On the lid of the loving-cup there is a man in armour. 'Tis not such loving-cups can bring peace on earth, good will among men, but only "He who took bread, and gave thanks and brake it, and gave unto them, saying, This is my body which is given for you : this do in remembrance of me. Likewise also the cup after supper, saying, This cup is the new testament in my blood which is shed for you."

PENZANCE, *Fri.* 21.—Having, although so near, not visited the Land's End, and not knowing, so uncertain is our life, whether I should again be permitted to visit this country, I yesterday set forth thither. On my way I turned aside to visit the Logan Stone, which, during my short stay at St. Buryan's, I had not opportunity to examine.

'Tis ninety tons or more in weight, and yet a child may rock it. Dr. Borlase, who hates the Methodists, but hath the repute of being a man of great learning in the antiquities of his county, is of opinion, I am told, that these Logan Stones (for there are more than one) were idols of the Druids, which those artful priests used by way of ordeal; affirming that though a touch of the innocent would move them, no force on the part of the guilty could make them budge an inch; and so ordering matters as to lock their motion, when any approached to touch on whom they would fix the charge of guilt.

'Tis marvellous how in times so rude masses so mighty were lifted to their places. *Were* the times of antiquity indeed as rude as they have been represented? May they not have had appliances of machinery of which we know nothing? Or again, may not these Logan Stones have been in the beginning part and parcel of the rocks on which they rest, and have been separated from them by the gradual action of the elements? But, instead of indulging in these vain speculations, he who loves everywhere to find his Saviour can make of these strange stones a type of the Rock of Ages, to which the feeblest hand is not outstretched in vain.

As we journeyed on, I was shown a rock with a split in it through which, say the Cornish folk, when a packhorse can pass with its panniers on, the end of the world will have come; and again a great stone, at which seven kings are said to have dined; and where, according to an idle and profane prophecy, still more will feast before the final burning. How lightly do fools speak of that last dread day, when the secrets of men's hearts shall be laid bare, and all be brought to judgment!

At the Land's End, my companion being a pious man, I fell upon my knees, and bowing my head upon a rock, I prayed earnestly that I might indeed be made pure in heart. Never before had I so felt that without purity none could see God. 'Twas as though I had been brought face to face with eternity. To right, to left, in front, a boundless sea, breaking in awful thunder on the granite crags. To-morrow I shall set out on the first stage of my journey in good earnest towards my home. I shall rest on the Sabbath at a pious friend's; but I would that I had so ordered matters that it had not delayed me on the road, but on the other hand that I might have spent it with my family. O Lord, watch over them, and grant, if it be according to Thy will, that I may again behold my beloved Hester in the flesh.

Fri. 28.—The heat being still great, I found my poor Hester as I left her, save with perhaps even less strength than she had (and that indeed was little), to enable her to bear her load. 'Tis very hard to watch the sufferings of those we love, and know that we can do nothing to lighten them. But nay, we can pray, and the Lord, who giveth exceedingly abundantly more than we can ask or think, in His own way answers prayer. In the depth of her bodily weakness, the dear child's faith hath never failed, but grown stronger as the poor flesh hath grown more feeble. The Lord's will be done. When I note her pain, and know her longings to depart, and how well prepared she is for the great change, I could almost pray for her release. But dear Patty cannot give her up. Methinks the loss of her sister will break the poor child's heart. O Lord, give us all grace and strength to submit to Thy will in all things. 'Tis ofttimes easier to strive to do it than endure it.

Fearing that if I loitered, I might not see my dear child alive, I rode fast on my return; but that even so I might not wholly neglect my Heavenly Father's business,

I distributed on my way little tracts, with which I had nigh stuffed my saddle bags. Some I scattered to be carried by the winds, like the thistledown that was floating abundantly about me, but freighted with more precious seed. When last with him, Mr. Wesley told me that on the National Fast Day in December, two years agone, "An Earnest Exhortation to Serious Repentance" was given to every person who came out of church in or near London, a copy being left at his door for every householder who had not attended church; and that he believes that on that day the Lord turned away His wrath from us. 'Twas the day on which the Duke's army escaped from the rebels' ambuscade on Clifton Moor. Their bullets came like hail from the hedges and walls behind which they lay, but scarce a dozen of our men were hit.

XXIII.

Sun. Aug. 30.

WHEN I left for Cornwall, our Society was again at peace, refreshing to my spirit as to a mariner a calm harbour after having been storm-tost on the ocean. But during my absence a young man, W. J., hath joined us, who is likely to breed strife once more. Although he lived in Bath, he must needs come out to us instead of continuing to unite himself with the brethren in the city. I shall make inquiry, and doubtless shall find that he hath sufficient reason, though not to his credit. He thinks that he hath a fine voice (but in this he deceives himself), bringing in among us, instead of sober melodies, outlandish airs (which, sure, must be of his own composing), and indulging in most fantastic flourishes. Verily Mr. Wesley would have good cause for his saying that he never relished a tune at first hearing, if he heard W. J.'s. But had I not had it from his own lips, I had not thought

Mr. Wesley so fickle as he affirms himself to be concerning tunes and other matters. He says that never tune at first hearing, poem at first reading, face or picture at first sight, yet pleased him : and that when they have grown pleasant through use, then straightway their favour in his eyes begins to fade.

Mon. 31.—'Tis as I thought ; W. J. was separated from the Society at Bath by Mr. Wesley, on the occasion of his last visit, because of his loose behaviour, and after indulging in it openly for awhile, hath again taken a pious fit, and come to fasten himself on us in ———. My master, I find, was his leader, and I am told would gladly have screened him, out of charity, as he said ; but I fear 'twas because of business dealings between them : eagerly answering, " Yea," when Mr. Wesley asked, in examining the classes, " Does this person go to church and use the other means of grace? Does he meet you as often as he has opportunity?" But when it came to, " Does he live in drunkenness or any other open sin?" Mr. Saunders was constrained to give up his friend. 'Tis strange that one with such a gift of prayer as Brother Saunders hath beyond dispute, should so oft by worldliness be led into crooked ways. Who can touch pitch and not be defiled ? Alas! sometimes I have been carried up, as it were, into heaven, while listening to his prayers, and then the thought of what I have that day heard from him in the counting-house, or overheard in the shop, hath suddenly brought me down to earth like a dropped stone or a bird shot in the midst of its rejoicing. This greed of gain at any cost is growing on him, to the great grief, as is manifest, of his good wife. O Lord, open Thou his eyes before it be too late. But this I will say for him that he never openly visits his displeasure on them whom he hath sounded and found disinclined to bend to his purposes; nay, is constrained, as it were, to show them more honour than to those who have taken his hints at dishonest behaviour. Thanks be unto the Lord, a good work is going on both in the shop and in the yard. Ten of the young men and youths meet daily to pray and search the Scriptures, diligently examining one the other therein. They deny themselves that they may give to the poor, and stir one another up to all manner of good works. And these of all are the most industrious in their worldly callings. Young Joyce is of them. His poor father is again walking as becometh a Christian. The man at the Blue Boar hath much to answer for in tempting him back to the sin which doth most easily beset him. Fitly might he be called the Man of Sin. The blood of how many a soul will the Lord require at his hand! Good Sayers daily grows in grace. Jacky is much with him; for there is no gloom in his religion, and he is full of devices for the entertainment of the little lad whom he saved from drowning. Methinks that the little Susan is somewhat jealous of the love which the two have for one another, and the time they pass together. More than ever she nestles to me now that she hath not so much of her brother as she had. But Jacky, who likewise is of a jealous disposition, on coming in, will (though he dearly loves his sister) strive to crowd her from my knee, or, at the worst, to get the nearer place. 'Tis droll to note the little lad's lyings in wait to get the first kiss from his mother and myself, and his runnings back to get the last. Sayers tells me that Jacky hath a brain beyond the common for mechanical contrivance, and works willingly at odd hours to carry out my boy's designs.

Sun. Sept. 6.—This hath been a sad, clouded day, for my poor Patty; but, thank God, at evening time there was light. Dear Hetty hath long urged her to communicate, but she hath shrunk from so doing through a sense of unworthiness, citing in reply to her sister's remonstrances that Scripture, " Wherefore, whosoever shall eat this bread and drink this cup of the Lord unworthily, shall be guilty of the body and blood of the Lord. But let a man examine himself, and so let him eat of that bread and drink of that cup. For he that eateth and drinketh unworthily, eateth and drinketh damnation to himself, not discerning the Lord's body."

I verily believe that the dear girl is a true child of God, but not being able to name the very hour in which the Lord spake peace to her soul, she shrank from approaching His table through dread of bringing condemnation on herself for unworthiness.

Having been persuaded by Hester to speak to the poor child (before I had abstained, feeling it safe to leave her in the hands of the Lord), I pointed out that in ancient times everyone who was baptised communicated daily ("They all continued daily in the breaking of bread, and in prayer"), and that though afterward a notion arose that 'twas not a converting but a confirming ordinance, in which none but they who had consciously received the Holy Ghost should participate, yet that this was false, experience did manifestly prove; many persons having been converted at the Lord's Supper. Moreover, when He instituted the ordinance, our Lord bade men who had not yet received the Holy Spirit, "do this in remembrance of me," and Himself, before the Holy Ghost was given unto them, administered to them the sacred elements. Accordingly, giving heed to my words, but still with much misgiving, poor Patty went this morning to the communion table; but when the cup was given to her, her hand shaking in her agitation, and it being filled too high, a little of the wine was spilt. Thereupon, Satan hissed into her ears that for her Christ's blood was shed in vain, and for hours she hath been in a horror of great darkness. But I thank the Lord, He hath heard our prayers, and she hath gone to her bed in peace. The coverlet was wet with her bitter tears.

Mon. 7.—This morning, the carrier with whom I formerly had talk overtook me on the road to Bath. Praise be to God, his heart is changed. He is now a Christian in deed, and not in word only, a doer, and not a hearer only of the word. As I listened to his blessed experience, whilst his front horse jingled on, that Scripture was brought to my mind, "In that day shall there be upon the bells of the horses HOLINESS UNTO THE LORD."

Thurs. 10.—This day, at noon, Mr. Wesley preached at Bath. Mr. Saunders could not find time to go, and gave me charge of his wife. Not only the ten who make an open profession of religion, but most of the other servants, gave up their dinner hour to hear the sermon. Before starting for Bearfield, Mr. W. rode over to visit my Hetty. I found her much comforted by his words; and dear Patty likewise. He is never more like Christ than in his manner to young women. 'Tis no wonder they love him.

Sat. 19.—The crispness of the air, without cold, hath given dear Hetty some relief from the excess of her languor. But 'tis plain now that she cannot much longer tarry with us. She knows it. Nevertheless, her heart is as still as the sunny silent land around, wherein, although the unwagging leaves still hang thick, and many are scarce changed in colour, save that they are darker than in spring, nevertheless, they seem to know that they are soon to fall. 'Tis poor Patty now that is troubled. As she works by her sister's bed she looks up from her stitching, and when she notes her sister's quiet face, or with a smile on it for her, the tears are ever coming to her eyes; and when Hetty falls asleep, the poor child softly, yet swiftly, slips from the room to vent her grief in private. Even the middle-aged, nay, those with one foot in the grave, find it hard to bring death home to themselves. No wonder to the young, their own death, or the death of any they love, is a thing nigh incomprehensible. Joan and Frances, wondering, asked me why their sister wept; and when I told them, they burst into as passionate a flood of tears. Although Hetty hath been daily sinking before their eyes, 'twas the first time that they had thought that she could die.

Tues. Oct. 27.—Mistress Saunders hath lent me "Some Remarkable Passages in the Life of Colonel James Gardiner," by that good man Dr. Philip Doddridge, whom I fain would have seen at Northampton. 'Tis a book that I could but read at a sitting, remembering how we were in the North when that brave officer fell. In him, as in our dragoons, 'tis shown that Christians are no cowards, but the best of soldiers. Before the battle he gave Christian counsel to his servants, and then betook himself to prayer behind a barley rick. At the first onset he was wounded, and yet again, but he still fought on, although his men fled, save two officers and fifteen of his troopers, who stood by him to the last. 'Twas in heading a party of foot left without a leader, that he was cut down by a scythe fastened to a pole (such barbarian weapons did the savage Scots use), being afterwards brained by a broadsword, or Lochaber axe. His last thought was for his faithful servant, waving his hat and calling to him to take care of himself and retreat. Jacky hath eagerly listened to the account of the battle, expressing great indignation that Englishmen should be such cowards as to run away from savages, leaving behind them so brave an officer to be slain.

But to me the account of his conversion is the great thing of the book. Although all conversions be miraculous, yet was his so in an especial manner. While whiling away the time before the hour appointed for a deed of sin, the Lord upon the cross appeared unto him in a blaze of glory, and audibly reproached him for his shameful ingratitude. "O sinner, did I suffer this for thee, and are these thy returns?"

Sat. Nov. 28.—Mr. Wesley hath sent me an affecting

narrative. He hath been visiting M. C., a poor woman who, after having led a life of luxury as a kept mistress, when conviction of sin had come upon her at West Street chapel, at once betook herself to honest labour, "choosing rather to suffer affliction with the people of God, than to enjoy the pleasures of sin for a season." All the surplus of her wages she gave to the poor. Mr. Wesley having found her in dying circumstances and deep poverty, owing to long illness, mentioned her case to a benevolent lady, who sent her half a guinea. Thereupon M. sent for a baker to whom she owed as much, and would have had him take it, but the man, though poor, refused, saying that she stood more in need of it than he; and could not be prevailed upon to accept it, though his due, until M. told him that if he did not she could not die in peace. Mr. Wesley, still further to ease her mind, hath promised, after her death, to take charge of her child, a girl of eight, who hath no other friend.

I had not designed that my poor Patty should be made acquainted with this account, but chanced to leave the letter in my daughters' chamber, where Patty lighting upon it, took it up and read it, Mr. Wesley's letters having hitherto been looked upon as common property in our family. Dear girl, she hath prayed me to write to Mr. Wesley, begging him to suffer her to contribute yearly of her earnings towards the support of the child.

Mon. 30.—This morning, shortly after sunrise, our beloved Hester entered into the rest that remaineth for the people of God. The Lord gave, and the Lord hath taken away: Blessed be the name of the Lord. Fain would I say so with my whole heart, but, O my Father, the blow is hard to bear.

Sat. Dec. 5.—To-day we committed the mortal remains of our dear one to the dust. In spite of the rain and melting snow, there was a great gathering in the churchyard. The neighbours have been exceeding kind. Mr. Saunders came over to follow my dear child to the grave, and hath defrayed all the expenses of the funeral and the mourning. Good Mistress Saunders sat with my dear wife and girls, whilst I and little Jacky were away. Although the little lad sobbed as though his heart would break, nevertheless, he took pride in his long band and black cloak, and in walking with me as a chief mourner next after the coffin; and the little Susan looked at him through her tears as if proud that he should so play the man.

For the first time since I have been here, the Vicar showed a friendly disposition. He read the service with a gravity most unlike his usual gabble, and lingered afterward by the grave to say a word of kindness to me. 'Twas in his rough way, but, nevertheless, being manifestly sincere, 'twas a comfort unto me.

Thurs. 10.—My mind being somewhat more composed, I will now write down the particulars of our beloved Hetty's triumphant death. 'Twas her dear mother's turn to sit up with her; but Patty, although nigh worn out by her day's toil and nursing, would fain have taken her place. At her sister's wish she undressed and went to her bed, but not being able to sleep, after midnight she arose, and putting a shawl about her, seated herself beside her sister's. Hetty appeared glad to see her back, and from time to time, at a sign from her sister, Patty knelt down beside the bed and prayed aloud, to the great comfort of Hetty, but the astonishment of their dear mother. More than once both Patty and my wife, thinking that the end drew nigh, would have called us, but Hetty shook her head, and would not have us disturbed.

But when the house had begun to stir, Patty came hastily to summon us, and we hurried to the chamber. For a time our dear one took no notice of us. The last sands of her life seemed to be fast running out.

But shortly after the sun came up, her eyes opened, and noting the growing light, she motioned for the window-curtain to be drawn aside. 'Twas a morning strangely bright and calm for the end of November. The sunbeams made the long-wicked candles look dimmer than before, but lighted up our dear one's wasted face. But brighter than their light was the smile upon it. Our dear girl beckoned to us to come and say goodbye, and beginning at the youngest, we all went to receive her farewell kiss. To all she tried to say something, but at times her breath failed her. To her mother she said, "Dear mamma, seek Christ that we may meet again." Her parting with poor Patty was exceeding touching. When she had bidden us all good-bye, she looked up, like Stephen, stedfastly towards heaven; its glory seemed to be reflected in her face; and murmuring, "Lord Jesus, receive my spirit," she fell asleep.

The other children, although quietly, have begun to go about their occupations as before; but to Patty the death of her sister is a blow from which I greatly fear the dear child may never recover. O God, my Father, spare her to us! Though so many be left, the house is dreary, lonely.

THE END.

www.ingramcontent.com/pod-product-compliance
Lightning Source LLC
Chambersburg PA
CBHW031906220426

43663CB00006B/791